Wired Thoughts

D R Dixon

Published by Jenliss Publishing 2016

www.wiredthoughts.com

Book design and layout by Clare Brayshaw

Cover image by Conrad Marks

A CIP catalogue record is available for this title from the British Library.

ISBN 978-0-9934273-0-5 (Paperback)
ISBN 978-0-9934273-1-2 (Mobi)
ISBN 978-0-9934273-2-9 (ePub)

Prepared and printed by:

York Publishing Services Ltd
64 Hallfield Road
Layerthorpe
York YO31 7ZQ

Tel: 01904 431213

Website: www.yps-publishing.co.uk

Contents

Under a disguise

And another thing

This book is like taking a trip down memory lane or travelling back in time. It will take you to places you had forgotten existed. Memories that you had buried long ago in the depths of your mind will come rushing forward and present themselves to you once again. Some, you will greet like old long lost friends, smiling, laughing, feeling love and compassion. Others will make you cower at their return like an unexpected enemy at the door, here to play with your heartstrings and make you face your own feelings of hatred, jealousy and anger. This is a warts and all account of humankind and it makes no apologies for this and pulls no punches; you will just have to deal with it. Once you have endured the emotional highs and lows, this fascinating piece of work will leave you with an enormous sense of hope, belief and a realisation that destiny truly, is in your own hands.

Dean Powell

Dedication

This book is dedicated to those who have lost their way.

This book is dedicated to those who have become tired and question if it is simply too late.

This book is dedicated to those who know all they need is one chance, just one more genuine chance, to be able to turn things around and begin to create for themselves the life they have always wanted.

This book is dedicated to you.

Acknowledgements

I'd like to extend a big thank you to my cousin for his much appreciated support. Many of the thoughts I had and concepts which came to me arose out of the conversations we have had about life over the years. I constantly bombarded him with ideas. Sorry, but you proved to have a good listening ear. I should also say thank you to my daughters who also had no choice but to hear me out. Thank you for your strong words of encouragement. You believed in me from the beginning and told me I had something that people would want to hear, which only sharpened my determination to get this book out into the public arena. Thank You for providing the spark to ignite the fire within me.

I would also like to thank my mother, for instilling in me a hard work ethic.

And a special thank you to my partner for just being there when so much of my mind and attention was consumed in the making of *Wired Thoughts*. Last but probably most important of all I would like to say thank you to God for his guidance in making all of this possible.

To The Reader

Wired Thoughts is a collection, or if you like, an assortment of thoughts and ideas I have put together to address some of the problems and difficulties we may face in our everyday lives. The passages often contain powerful, inspirational, messages. The book illustrates, and goes into great depth and detail capturing, many of the ups and downs we all encounter on a day to day basis. The content can at times be tragic, but there are also elements of humour and a see-saw of emotions.

I hope this book will allow you to analyse and think about your own personal circumstances, as well as those of others around you. It may be that someone is in a predicament and unsure of what to do, in which case they may find an answer within these pages. This is really what I set out to do when I started this project – to put something down that people might recognise within themselves or see in something that a friend or relative may be going through; or just to offer some escapism. I wanted to produce something which was raw, no holds barred, and thought provoking. I wanted to bring stories to life that would have the reader eager to know what was going to happen next to the characters within them.

The purpose of my book is to draw the reader in, only for them to find out I am really shining a flashlight into their own lives, and by the time this has occurred I will have hopefully knocked them off balance and left them with some food for thought. I hope you enjoy the journey. Buckle up tight!

D R Dixon

Loss

Gone but not forgotten

I wish I had told her how much she meant to me. I wish I had. That's the one thing that will haunt me for ever. I could have said something and I never did, I never did. I loved her so much and now it's too late because she is gone, gone for ever, and I never told her. I can't believe it.

Life seems impossible without you, Mum. It's just not the same. It just isn't. I keep hearing your voice, seeing your image. Sometimes I go to pick up the phone to ring you. I even go to dial your number. The truth is, I'm not coping very well at the moment. I know you wouldn't want me to be like this but I can't help it, I just feel like I'm in a thick fog and I can't get out. I've got no energy to give David or the kids. I haven't even got energy for myself. Of course, he doesn't understand. He just tells me to pull myself together. He is so insensitive at times. I can't speak to him about how I'm feeling because he thinks I should be okay by now. But it has only been twelve months. I need him more than ever right now and he's just not here for me. The only time I've ever really needed him and I can't count on him.

I'm just blown away with it all and it's getting worse because it's coming up to the anniversary of the day when we lost you. I know I'm going to cry buckets on that day, but I'll try to think about the good memories, your sense of humour, and the happy times we shared. Like when our

Amanda went outside to put the rubbish out and we locked the back door behind her and we were killing ourselves laughing at her being outside in front of that workman, Steve, whom she fancied, with that stupid shower cap on and those ridiculous looking pyjamas. Or, I'll think about the time when we went to Alphie's party and Bridget was so pissed she was on the dance floor doing robotics and we were doubled over in stitches. Or the simple things like Friday nights getting a takeaway from Mr Wan's. That was your favourite and us watching an episode of *Friends* together.

And now you're gone, I even think about the pearls of wisdom you used to try to give to me. I used to call it nagging back then but the penny has finally dropped, Mum, and it all makes sense now. I'm grateful for all the things you did for me, and that even with all the stress I caused you, you never turned your back on me, no matter how much I screwed up. The memories I have of you, I shall treasure for ever. And something else that has stayed with me, going through all of this in the last twelve months, is that so often the thoughts we have just stay in our heads, but what good is that?

We all have someone we care about. Don't delay telling them how you feel or you'll end up in the same position as me. Write to them, knock on their door, do whatever it takes. Do it now, because when it's too late, well it's too late isn't it?

One day

André Augustine worked all the hours that God could send. He had just built his new home in France and was putting in the finishing touches. Now his new life could begin. He had earned it. He was selling up and leaving the UK. He and his wife were finally going to start enjoying life; he had worked non-stop and flat-out for the last ten years, seven days a week, and was looking forward to his retirement. That's when he was going to relax, take his foot of the gas, and have a new beginning.

He hadn't had much of a life. His wife had kept saying to him, "We need to do things together, André. We cannot let years and years pass without going anywhere, and having real quality time together." At last he'd been able to say, "Look, I am retiring in six months, I will only be fifty-three, and we will have the rest of our lives to have happy times. Don't you understand this is why I have been working so hard for the last ten years, so that we can have that time together?"

But after retiring from work and on the very day he was to fly out to France, André had a massive heart attack and died. No one could believe it; he'd looked like a picture of good health. His wife was devastated. They had not done anything together for a decade because every penny and André's every thought had been about moving to France. It had turned into an obsession. André would not enjoy himself, even a little, until he was retired and in France; he would not watch the movies he liked, he would not see the friends he liked, or do anything else he liked. Sadly, his wife felt cheated; they had put their whole life together on hold, for what seemed like an eternity, and now he was gone.

You can plan and plan for a day that isn't promised to you, or you can do the things you want to do and start living your life now.

The funeral

My dad never featured in my life. Other kids had their dad at home. I always wondered why my dad never came to see me. I know he was a bit of a ladies' man and shit happens. He and my mum didn't work out, for whatever reason. That's life, but why he never wanted to see me hurt, to be honest. Everyone in the family knew he never gave a shit about his kids. There were three of us altogether, all with different women, but his three true loves were alcohol, gambling and more alcohol. His kids didn't get a look in. Listen, if you want me to tell you a fairy tale, I will, but that's how it actually was. After hitting the bottle for years and years and hardly eating, his lifestyle finally took its toll and he died at the age of fifty-six.

I remember my uncle, with whom I'd always got on very well, saying, "Now Martin, how are you going to pay for your dad's funeral, because I don't see why I should, given that he was your dad and he hasn't left a penny to pay for anything!" I couldn't believe it. He'd never been there for me all my life and now I was being told that it was my debt, mine, and my brother and sister's whom he never saw either. No one had any money. I certainly didn't. There were lots of family get-togethers to work out how it could be paid for and who should pay what proportion. Everyone was frantically trying to find out if he had a pension or not. No one wanted to be lumbered with the bill. Everybody sighed a breath of relief when it turned out he had paid into a pension at some point in his life. And there was enough to cover the cost of his funeral: it would have been a cruel joke if we'd have had to foot the bill considering he was never there for us. We all started to calm down a bit.

Then a lot of people started getting in touch, cousins, long-lost relatives, some I'd never heard of before. Everyone was keeping their distance though. But as soon as the funeral was paid for everything changed. They all wanted to know if my dad had left any substantial money and who stood to get it. There were loads of arguments about it and accusations about money being stolen and hidden and people not getting their rightful share. I don't know what planet some of them were living on to think my dad was a secret millionaire. It was laughable. He was a hard core drinker and gambler. Nonetheless, all the vultures came swarming out of the woodwork looking for a pay-out. It was very undignified, in fact it was ugly. I didn't care about all that, my dad had just died. I guess someone passing away can bring out the worst in people. My uncle fell out with my aunt, my aunt fell out with my sister who in turn fell out with my cousin. My cousin fell out with my mum. There were massive ding-dongs the entire time. Aunty Susan wasn't talking to Uncle Ronald. Uncle Ronald wasn't talking to his brother Peter, and so on and so on. It was fucking ridiculous!

On the day of the funeral, the vicar said something in Church about events in my dad's life that made everyone smile as they could actually hear uplifting things about him. In fact, my uncle said some things too. He thanked everyone for attending and lending their support and said my dad would have been very proud of the turn-out. He also said we were a close-knit family, who would be there for each other in this time of sorrow. Well, that didn't sound at all like all the squabbling that had taken place behind the scenes. But no one was to know, that's a private matter. I mean, before it was discovered that my dad had a pension, they were all saying bad things about him. No one mentioned that in their tribute speeches. He had a good send-off though and everyone had a drink to his memory at the wake, the one place where it is acceptable to say what you really think. In fact Cousin Ollie said too much. He said my dad was a complete tosser, who still owed him £500 from twenty years before when he fixed a car for him. He was blind drunk, in fact he had to be dragged out of the building. There's always someone at these functions isn't there?

If I knew anyone who was going through anything like this, I think the one thing I'd say to them is, don't make it about yourselves, it's about the deceased. Don't fight each other and rip each other apart or say things you'll regret. How do you think your loved ones would feel to see you behaving like that?

Be there for each other, support each other, make time for each other and, above all else, remember your family, come together and pay your final respects.

Sink or swim

Sink or swim in this life – you can't do both, so you'd better make your mind up. Which one is it going to be? The choice is yours. Imagine being in so much turmoil, that the only way out was to take your life – suicide. Things would have to be pretty bad. Hey, I mean the pain would have to be unmeasurable, on the scale of something you can't comprehend, to do that. I mean, that's it, you can't change that. That's it, goodbye world, goodbye everything, all connections, relatives, loved ones, see ya! The final straw. But this story is far from finished. Because what you've done has just become apparent, there was confusion at first.

"No, he can't have done that! No, she can't have done that, she wouldn't do that, she's got two little children that depend on her for everything!" Think again. It's tragic because she did, she hung herself from the landing on top of the steps. Her nine-year-old daughter found her. She was a greyish colour. And I don't wanna give too much of a descriptive picture, but that image of her hanging from that bannister will haunt that little girl for the rest of her life. Still, she left her a little note that can be read in five seconds, to explain why she did it. So that's okay isn't it?

Why did you do it? Why did she do it? Her little girl had to go live with her poor grandma along with her four-year-old sister because they didn't have a mummy now. Grandma had to adopt the children, at her age as well, and in her failing health – all emotion sucked out of her. Expected to give and show the children the love they needed when she was now a walking zombie herself, crushed by the recent events, with the thunderbolt she had received, everything safe around her vanished. The disbelief at what her daughter had done ran havoc with friends, work colleagues, teachers from the kiddies' schools, with everyone who knew her! No one could believe it really, just deep shock, numbness. She was the last person you would expect to do something like that. It just left a gaping hole.

Her mum was never the same again. She suffered from bouts of depression. They say it totally affected her. After that day she never really smiled again. It was horrendous. Eventually, her depression just got stronger and stronger. The tablets stopped working and in the end she had to be hospitalised. The two little kids had to be put into care.

It's not just about the person who commits the act, is it? What about those who are left behind to pick up the pieces? Those who have no choice, but to pick up the shattered pieces left behind by a daughter, mother, brother, sister, aunty, dad, uncle? What about those who have to deal with it all, how do they move on? Maybe they never do!

Your life is connected to many other lives, so if you commit suicide your suffering may come to an end, but for others their suffering will only just be beginning.

Death we must accept it

Death, you have to accept it, you can't change it so what's the point? You can't stop living just because someone has died – where will it get you? You can insist on refusing to accept the passing of a loved one by punishing yourself by refusing to eat drink or sleep, by standing still and choosing not to move forward by telling yourself nothing matters any more; maybe guilt has you over a barrel because you never made peace with them before they passed or said the things you wanted to and now you feel ill because you have missed the opportunity to do so. You can stop doing everything you to need to do; you can stop going to work, looking after yourself, dressing your children but it won't help you. It's the law of nature from the moment we are conceived. All that we do ultimately leads one day to that moment. We know just like there's a beginning, there has to be an end. Remember the good times, focus on those. Keep yourself busy, stay active, do what you have to do, but you must accept it.

No one escapes that path: the Lord giveth and the Lord taketh away. Death is as natural as life and vice versa, they work hand in hand together. If you want to stop living because of the loss of a loved one, you are not understanding how the universe works. Grieve for your loved one, be sad. But do not remove yourself from the living. The days will get easier in time and you will feel stronger, because you will have accepted that after death comes life and after life comes death.

If you accept what has happened, you will rise again.

Man, God, The Devil and Religion

Mrs X

Mrs X is a strong figure in the church. She rarely smiles and always appears to be bothered by the sound of young babies, and children making a noise and not sitting up straight and proper during hymn singing. She organises a lot of the evening tea events for the church that are usually well attended. Only thing is, at these events, Mrs X seems to spend most of her time discussing the private lives of the congregation. For instance, she called Mrs Jones a "complete whore" who just about everyone had slept with at some time or another. And she called the woman's daughter Cindy another man-hungry slut who had also sat on everybody's dick. She also said the only reason why Dave Smith had stayed with his wife Felicity was because he wanted the money out of her savings. And she called Paul Taylor, who is a lovely, gentle man, a faggot who, on the day of reckoning, would burn in hell for his homosexual deeds. She had something to say about everybody and occasionally her husband, Mr X, would provide even more intimate detail, if it was required.

For over twenty-five years, Mrs X had been walking to the church, half a mile, limping with her walking stick, a feat which she was proud of and one which was praised by many churchgoers who admired how this lady suffered pain to go and pray before her saviour. But in all those years, she never learned a single lesson from all her prayers, Bible readings and all the hymns she sang. In fact, I can't think of a more unholy person. It's a pity 'cause there are a lot of Mr and Mrs Xs that wrap themselves up in the cloth of God and sit down in church every week, every Sunday, and miss absolutely everything, week in and week out, and go back to their same despicable behaviour the minute the service has finished – their envying, their loathing, their selfishness. They never seem to peer into the mirror and take a good look at themselves.

Mrs X finally passed away when she was eighty-four years old. They had a special memorial service at the church. When her name was mentioned, they described her as having been a fount of wisdom and a pillar of the community, and one of the kindest, warmest individuals to have ever walked the planet. The church even received its biggest amount in donations in over ten years on that day. There was a minute of silence in which she was honoured. There were tears and people breaking down everywhere as everyone celebrated her life and paid homage to her memory, the way she had lived her life with such grace and integrity. Yes, Mrs X was a God-fearing woman and she would be sadly missed by everyone!

The Devil whisperer

When the Devil whispered in my ear I tried to ignore him. But he can be pretty convincing. He told me I could have extramarital sex and it would be fine, no one would need to know. He had penetrated my mind. I tried to fight him, but I couldn't, he was too persuasive. Still, I was eighty per cent good.

He came to me again and told me to have more fun. I did this time; it was with my brother's wife. I had never noticed her before in that way. Why would I, she was my brother's wife? They had always been happy, but the Devil whispered in my ear and told me she was mine for the taking, so I took her. I brought her to orgasm, then I was done with her. I did not think about their relationship, I did not think about them. I did not think about anything.

The Devil whisperer told me about the money I could get which was just there for the taking. So I committed fraud on a frightening scale. No one knew, and I got away with it. I had no remorse and no regrets. He said I deserved it. Then I was only fifty per cent good.

He kept coming to me, he knew I was weak by the time he had finished with me. There was nothing good left. I had followed his every instruction to the letter, I was all bad and out of control, all that was good had vanished. There were no traces left. I had served him so well that he now allowed me to do the whispering, he asked me to convert others into darkness and I did, me and my followers, but there were some we couldn't convert.

If you don't listen, we can't change you.

Forgive me

Forgive me Lord for I have sinned. Everything I touched, I broke. Everything I held dear to me, I destroyed. Everything in my path, which was good, became bad. I wrack my brain to think where on my journey I became lost. What ignited the flame? What was it? You cannot lie to yourself. God is the truth. Your conscience is the truth. At the end of the day, that will be your biggest battle. What is done in the dark, they say, will be revealed in the light. What is hidden shall be seen. The invisible will be visible. The sins perpetrated today will be unravelled tomorrow. I have first-hand knowledge of this because of sins I have committed.

I have a sickness in my body that grows every day. I am overpowered by its strength. On the outside, my appearance has not altered, but on the inside I am consumed with grief and guilt. Each day these feelings increase, the things I have done in this life, things I am deeply ashamed of, some of which I could never repeat to a single human being. Lord, when I have done so much wrong, can I ask for forgiveness? Is that a futile request? I want to pray, but I am afraid you will turn me away. I want to kneel before you, but I am not worthy to do so. I want to confess everything, but there's too much to undo. I fear there's no room for me at your inn and my days are numbered. Please let me in!

Forgiving yourself is the beginning of the healing process.

Holy cloth

The priest from Church had been coming to our home to give my wife extra Bible lessons. I thought it was a good thing for her as she had recently lost her mother. Only one day I came home from work early and caught them in our bed together. I couldn't believe it. I had never once been suspicious, well, because he was a priest. But even the man in the holiest cloth is just a man. He took advantage of the situation and slept with my wife.

I said, "What about your God now?"

He said, "What about him?"

I said, "What about the sermons you gave at Church in front of hundreds of people about redemption, going to heaven and judgment day?" He said he was merely doing a job which his father had done before him. He said it was words, just words. He had not wanted to disappoint his father who had been a priest before him.

The priest was naked in bed with my wife. She was crying, probably because I had caught the pair of them red-handed. He still had his arms around her. They were both very sweaty and he was smiling at me. He stretched his hand out to me and said, "We are still going to be friends aren't we, old chap? You wouldn't hit a man of God would you?"

I said, "No, but I would hit you."

You'll just have to imagine what happened next.

All men are created in sin.

Conversations with God

It was a freezing cold night. My hands were trembling and tears were streaming from my eyes. I knew what I was going to do. I walked down to the Church, picked up the biggest brick I could see and hurled it through the window. I'd been drinking that day. I'd had a bottle of sherry. I was pretty fresh really, but I wanted to give him a piece of my mind, so I just smashed the window and went in. I switched the lights on and looked at that statue of Jesus and swore at him and cursed him for making me lose my job and taking my wife and children away from me and for a whole bunch of other things he had done to me and for leaving me with a big fat nothing. I was screaming, asking why he had done it to me, letting him have it for nearly an hour before I got it all out of my system.

I was just about to leave when a voice beckoned me to turn around. There was a blinding bright light. I could hardly see anything, but I knew instantly it was him (God). He told me he was going to break with tradition and for once, for my own good, was going to tell me some home truths. He said I didn't lose my job because of him. He said I lost my job because I had become lazy and wouldn't get up early enough in the morning to be there. He said somebody else had got my job. And he said my wife left me because I'd had numerous affairs behind her back and in the end she became tired of me and wanted a better life for herself. He said it had nothing to do with him.

I complained about my breathing problems and said if he was so magnificent, why had he created me like this? He said I had brought them on myself, that he had tried to help me and convince me to quit smoking. The time I ended up in hospital with a serious chest infection was him trying to warn me about the dangers of smoking, but I'd refused to take any notice. He said he was sick of people blaming him and making him a scapegoat for all of their problems and only coming to him when they were in deep trouble and needed his help. He asked me if I was not glad my children were healthy and I told him that I was. He said I had the strength and determination to turn my life around from any situation, no matter how bad it seemed to be at the time. I told him I was happy about that. He continued to ask me question after question, over and over again. He kept talking to me like this and the more and more I listened, the more I understood and realised that my anger was mis-directed. It wasn't God who had given me all my problems, it was me.

We can't do it without him

We can't do it without him. Those who do not believe are usually confused and lost in life. They do not acknowledge his existence. So what is real to them? Whom do they serve? No one. There is no higher presence for them, so it is no wonder when they fall on their own swords and self-destruct. We cannot do it without him. He will never turn his back on you, if you go to him. He will forgive you and welcome you to his home. I begged his forgiveness and told him I was ready when I went to his house. Many laughed. They said I was crazy, and I had suffered a nervous breakdown. But I was having a breakdown without him. My sins were limitless. His power made me whole again and restored my balance. God is everything. God is love and God is inside you. But you cannot do it without him.

To have faith, you just have to have faith.

Love, sex and all that

What is it?

What is love? Why are we all looking for it? Why do we need it so much? What is the chemical formula for love? Why is it so important to us? What is its mathematical sign? Why do scientists say we can live a longer life if we have it and we will live a shorter, lonely, existence without it? If you are not in receipt of love, are you only half a person without it? What does love mean to you? Can you explain it? Take a look at the person you have chosen to be your partner. Do it discreetly though, do not let them notice what you are doing. Just think about it. Now think about it deeply. Now focus. Do they fill you with love? What do they fill you with? If it's not love, then maybe you found something else, maybe that person is taking happiness away from you. It's true people fall in and out of love all the time, but then they still want love again even if they have been badly bruised, because they still believe love is attainable, because they still believe love can fill them up. Love has been around as long as the earth has been rotating. You can do magical things if you have love. You can elevate to a higher plane and do unimaginable, delightful things.

Love is precious. Love is all that matters and when it comes down to it, it's all you really need. You need to find love.

Somebody else

I've been with Rhonda for nine years now, but she's just not you. I do love her, but she's not you. We could have had a happy life together, you and I, had you given us a chance, had you come to me. I waited and waited for you to end it with him, but you didn't. I started seeing you, because you told me how unhappy you were with him and I fell in love with you. It wasn't about sex. For the first time in years, I felt alive and happy again. I hated waiting to hear from you. I'd look at my phone constantly, just hoping you would send me a message some days, and when you didn't I would feel sad. I couldn't contact you, because of our circumstances, because of him.

The very last time we slept together, I told you I couldn't do it any more. It was causing me too much pain not being with you, having snatched moments together, it was too much for me. I wanted you to feel how I felt. I tried to make you see we should be together, that you would miss me. I tried to give you an ultimatum, it didn't work. You said you were unhappy, but you stayed with him. I would have done anything for you, anything, she is a good person my Rhonda, but there's no point in lying, she's just not you.

We grew into love. There wasn't an instant attraction, we were both at a loose end when we met. We had both been through hell and back. We had both experienced loneliness and that was the foundation of our relationship. We settled together and we were doing okay. Then I heard you had split up with him. I couldn't believe it... what I had wanted all along had happened. But now, I was with someone I didn't want to be with, but I couldn't just turn my back on Rhonda, because no matter what, I still had feelings for her.

Then you went to Greece. I received a letter from you telling me you had found work over there and you had met someone. But then soon afterwards you told me your new boyfriend had been sleeping around, you had found out about it, and now you were going to be coming back home. It's brought up the old feelings I had for you. Again, my head's been spinning, wondering what it would be like if we were together, but I'm still with Rhonda and I do love her. You're the greatest love that never happened.

You can spend all your time dreaming of the person you wish you were with or you can be present with the person who you are with.

Stolen moments

Hey, you two. Yeah, I'm talking to you two. What are you both playing at? You're both in a relationship. In fact you, you're married, and you, you've got a baby at home. Do you think a couple of snatched hours a week qualify you as the world's greatest lovers? An hour in the back seat of a car or in some sleazy hotel? What are you going to do when everything leaks out? Oh and by the way it always leaks out, ask anyone who's been in your situation.

What are you going to do then, when you lose your girlfriend and new born baby? Or what will you do, when you lose your husband and your fancy lifestyle? Are you both going to console each other? Let's have a look at the likelihood of that. What do you even know about each other apart from that she can give a dirty blow job and make you scream like Michael Jackson? Do you even know if she can fry an egg? And do you know that the money he spends on you comes from his girlfriend's savings account? What do you really know about each other apart from the obvious?

I've got news for you. You're so close to falling off the cliff right now. The other day you were both spotted together in your car, Lorraine – or should I say your husband's car – by Malcolm, your neighbour. He saw you, in the morning when you were supposed to be at work, and another man was in the car with you, that other man would be you, Tom. Well Malcolm noticed. You both looked very cosy together and he thought he saw you kissing. Well, ever since, he has been itching to have a word with your husband. He is going to be very subtle about it and ask him about the hours you work, whilst he tells him about his greenhouse. He has never liked your husband since he criticised some flowers he planted a year ago and said they weren't very good. So he would love to be the bearer of bad news. But, he isn't the only one who is suspicious.

Tom, you're not in the clear either. Your girlfriend has been going through all your belongings, including your mobile phone, for the last three weeks, looking for evidence that you are messing' around. She tells her sister something isn't right, she can't put her finger on it, but something smells funny. You're acting out of character. Well we know why that is don't we? It's because when you've come home from seeing Lorraine you're so paranoid she will be able to detect the smell of perfume or sex on you, that you go straight upstairs to hit the shower before you even say hello. She is so onto you.

Her sister has been giving her lots of support, encouraging her to keep checking on you until you slip up, so it's only a matter of time really, Tom, Tom, Tom, Tom, dear Tom. After you've dragged everyone through the wreckage, when everything comes out into the open, you two young lovebirds are going to be fine aren't you, when you lose everything? I wonder if those great blow jobs that Lorraine can give will be enough to replace the loss of your son, because your partner Chloe will probably move back to Australia. After all, she was just staying in England because you talked her into settling over here.

And your husband, Lorraine, will no doubt cut you off without a penny, so you will probably lose your lavish lifestyle. But that doesn't matter, you two really connect, that's the important thing. You will be able to get a place of your own and build a new life together, because you know so much about each other. It should be a walk in the park really, yes I can see it all so clearly, and you'll have no problems at all.

Proof is in the pudding

I told Sandra I didn't know Wayne had been seeing her and that he had been two-timing us both, playing us for fools. She called me a liar. Wayne had said I was a madwoman and I was jealous of their relationship and I wanted to split them up and Sandra believed him.

Twelve months I'd been seeing the bastard and he denied everything. Coming to my house, sleeping with me. I was very bitter and upset. Who wouldn't have been? I just thought *silly bitch, I'll prove it to you*. That's when the idea came to me: I'll stop taking the pill. There will be no way on earth he'll be able to talk himself out of that one. So I sent him a saucy text one night saying my mouth was dry and I needed a big big lolly to suck and did he know where I could get one? I got no reply, but I didn't give up.

A couple of days later I sent another one, saying I was thinking about him, I didn't have any panties on and I was feeling so horny. My phone started ringing immediately. It was Wayne, he told me basically he had too much at stake, he didn't want to lose Sandra and their baby and he apologised for not telling me he was in a relationship when we met. I told him not to worry, I knew where I stood now. He could still see me and still see Sandra if he wanted. I set the bait for him. I know what men are like.

A week later, I got a text from him. He asked what I was doing. I said nothing, that I was bored and frustrated, that I had a mini-skirt on and some thigh-high boots, and I was ever so bored. I had hardly put the phone down when he was banging at the door. As soon as I opened it, we started to make out. We were kissing, he was grabbing my hair and I was sticking my tongue in and out of his mouth and I thought *You lying bastard, I'm going to get pregnant and have your baby and we'll see what your girlfriend thinks then. Seeing as though I'm such a lying slag.* I rode down on him with all my strength. I thought I was going to break it off. We were like that then at least three or four nights a week. I thought *I'll prove you've been lying.*

A couple of months later, I found out I was pregnant. It hit me like a ton of bricks what I had just done. I told his girl, she couldn't argue with me then and the paternity test proved he was the dad and that I wasn't a liar. However she still stayed with him. He is still with her and their child, but he won't come and see mine. I got pregnant to prove to her he was sleeping with me and I wasn't a madwoman. When I think I didn't even want another baby, why did I do it? Sandra wasn't the only silly bitch.

We can create our own happiness and we can also create our own heartache.

Which way to turn

Philippa was a constant embarrassment for Harry. Whenever they went out, at the end of the night she would lose all her bearings and etiquette and usually be lying under the table she had been drinking at. This drove Harry crazy as he was a very proud man who expected a lady to behave like a lady at all times.

"Why do you do it? Why don't you know your limit?" he argued. "Why do you always have to get yourself in such a state? Why can't you realise when you've had too much, Philippa?" She would promise the morning after it would never happen again. She was going to change. But her determination would only last until the next time she was out and she would repeat the same behaviour. This made Harry furious, as he thought she was deliberately disregarding his feelings.

He started moving away from her. He stopped trusting her to do the right thing. He became guarded and upset when she would mention she was going out, because he knew what it meant; that she would lose all control and common sense and make a show of herself. He expected more from her. In return, his behaviour towards her, made her loathe him as she thought he was controlling and demanding. She liked getting out of control and having no restrictions. She told him she was an adult, free to do what she wanted. "So what if I fall over and I don't know who I am or where I am. I am still young." That in itself was a problem.

There was a twenty year age gap between Harry and Philippa. In the beginning, it hadn't seemed to matter. Now it did. Harry had already done many of the things Philippa was only just beginning to do.

"I want to enjoy life. Harry, what do I do? Why do you think I am such a bad person? I would never hurt you, I love you. I am loyal to you, why can't you love me the way I am, like I love you?" She couldn't see why Harry was so upset.

"I don't put any conditions on you. Don't put any on me. I will do as I please." They could not find any halfway territory, so the relationship was fraught with misunderstandings, innuendo and bad feeling. It seemed like they were just different people now, blaming each other for the reasons why things were going wrong. They had fallen in love once upon a time. In fact, they were still in love.

If you don't see eye to eye with your partner and you have unresolved issues that threaten your relationship, instead of trying to get your own point of view across, try listening, not talking, and either compromise or say goodbye. If you can't reach a compromise, you'll be saying goodbye anyway.

All's fair in love and war

All's fair in love and war Edward would say as went to bed with with his brother's fiancée, his cousin's wife and his best friend's soon-to-be wife. He had been an absolute scoundrel for years, but he changed his ways when he met Natasha and fell in love. Things were great for many years but then they soured and they went through difficult times.

Natasha met a kind man called Ralph Higgins who took her breath away. Ralph told her he had found love and married twenty years before, but his wife had an affair and she left him. Natasha liked Ralph and told him her own marriage to Edward was all but over and they started seeing each other. However she could not live with herself after a while and she summoned up the courage and told Edward all about Ralph.

When Edward saw them together, he realised to his surprise that Ralph was someone he had known when he was younger – they used to be friends. In fact Edward had slept with Ralph's wife during their marriage. Ralph told him to forget the past, that it was a long time ago and that he had moved on and fallen in love with Natasha. It wasn't for revenge, he said, as he'd had no idea she was married to Edward. He also told him all's fair in love and war.

So in love

We met in sunny Jamaica in Negril. I was on a beach. The view was fantastic and the sea was absolutely breathtaking. My friend Lucy and I were sunbathing. We were talking about what we planned to do that evening when out of nowhere he just appeared. He came up to me and asked what a lovely woman like me was doing on the beach, without a man to accompany me. I just laughed and asked him if he was blind. I didn't need a man and I wasn't on my own. Hadn't he noticed my friend Lucy right beside me? He smiled too and said he only saw me. My friend Lucy is drop-dead gorgeous, but he noticed me, not her. It was love at first sight. He called me his Marilyn Monroe.

I was sixty-one, he was twenty-one, but it didn't matter, we just hit it off. He took me out. From then on we spent every minute of our time together. I know it was difficult for Lucy, but I just wanted to be with him. When it was the last day of the holiday he broke down crying and said he wanted to come to England to look after me and he proposed to me.

My friends seemed to be jealous of us as they kept saying, "Watch out for him! Why does he want to get married so soon?" I cut them off. Jealousy, I have no time for it. We had a battle with immigration, but we decided to get married and we did so on his first day in England.

A few months later my heart was broken because he went missing. A vindictive friend told me her daughter saw him with another woman in London. She's never liked me – what a liar! Some people say he has taken advantage of me and led me up the garden path. I haven't heard a word from him for some time now, but I'm going to keep depositing money into his bank account to make sure he's okay. I'm worried about him. I don't care if it takes the rest of my life, as long as we can be together again. He's just had a touch of anxiety, I know that's all it is. I'm his Marilyn Monroe. I know what we had was true and for those people who say nasty things about him, all I can say is he loves me. They don't know about the bond we have between us. How can they? What do they know about anything? Some people don't have a clueeee. Do they?

Making do

You might be surprised, but my wife's been seeing her lover Adam now for the last thirty-six months. I've tried to help them out at times by making myself scarce. If your partner's attracted to someone else, you don't fight it, let it burn itself out. I didn't really like it when she brought him home to our bed though, I was a little bit upset about that, but deep down where it really matters I know she still loves me.

I've never mentioned anything to her about Adam even though I've known about it virtually from the start. I wouldn't want to cause any unnecessary distress. We have two kids you see. Why damage their lives, why hurt them? I just turn a blind eye to it. I understand she needs to be able to express herself, in maybe a different way than she can with me, and I've had to work away sometimes for a couple of weeks at a time.

In a way it's been my fault. As a Sales Agent, you see, I've had to travel up and down the country to earn my money so I know how lonely being apart can be and I can imagine how she must have felt. She's a lovely looking girl too. You should see her, I truly love her. She's the only one for me. I know you don't understand, how could you? I've been with her for twenty-two years for God's sake, so I'm not going to lose her to some slimy toe rag on a bunk up. I love her and she'll come to her senses in her own time, like she has done before. I'm not going to be a fool and throw away everything we've built up over the years. That would be stupid wouldn't it, to do that? We'll work it out and everything will come good. I'll book a holiday again and everything will be fine and we'll get back on track and everything will be smashing just like the good old days.

I've seen some people who have been through a divorce. All that drama, who gets the cat, splitting everything in half... it's horrible. No, a messy business divorce, definitely not for me. Besides, marriage is for better or for worse and I got married for life.

Still, if my old queen was still alive, she'd have something to say about it. She never liked June, she always said she'd never make me happy. I don't know, I've got a big house, a good job, we've got an outdoor swimming pool, holidays twice a year. So I don't think I've done too badly considering. Some people don't have half of the things that we have. Yes, if the good Lord was to give me another ten or twenty years of this, I'd be more than pleased.

Whatever you settle for is what you will get.

Baby talk

I'm not seeing your child. She's not mine. Find the real daddy, I'm nobody's fool, don't try to stick me with your baby. What do I look like? She doesn't have my ears, my nose, my build, nothing. I've got three other children and they all look exactly like me. So how can your baby be mine?

My mum said she's not ours, she's too light-skinned, her hair is all wrong. It's like a reddish colour. We don't have any red hair in our family tree. You're not pinning your baby on me, plus the dates you mentioned don't tally up. And I used protection, I always do... I'm sure I did.

'Are your assumptions based on what you think or scientific evidence? If you're not seeing your child because of how he or she looks, you could be making a huge mistake!'

A few months later, I had to let mum know. The results came through the post this morning and it's been confirmed 99.9 per cent the baby is mine. I was wrong and I've found out since that when two people have a baby, the attributes, features, appearance of the child can come from either parent. So the information I had was flawed.

Incidentally, as well, just for a bit of an update, my Uncle James had a look back through our family tree and discovered, unknown to us, that my great-great-grandma, Lavinia Smith, had the most unusual long bright fiery-red hair.

Love at the same heights

Sasha: I love you so much, I'd swim across the English Channel to be with you.

McKenzie: I love you too, but I couldn't possibly swim across the Channel to meet you, that's crazy.

Sasha: In fact, I love you so much I would walk on broken glass to be with you.

McKenzie: I love you too, but you can think again if you'd think I'd walk on broken glass for you.

Sasha: My love for you runs so deep, I would take a bullet for you if it would prevent you from suffering.

McKenzie: Thank you, that is very kind of you. I must admit I would put you in front of a bullet too to avoid being shot.

Try to fall in love with someone who loves you the same way you love them.

Don't leave me

Veronica said her life was over. She said there was nothing worth living for. Lionel didn't want her any more, he had made that clear. He'd had enough. She had tried to make it work, but he wanted out of the relationship. She was in total despair; she had just been told she was going to lose her job too. It was like everything that could go wrong was happening in real time and it was just one thing after another.

She had tried with Lionel, she really had. Her eyes had never wandered throughout their time together, but the same could not be said of him. He'd had countless affairs, he was both ignorant and arrogant and he rarely considered her feelings, yet she was the one who was falling apart, begging for forgiveness. To onlookers, this was strange because most people thought she would be glad it was finally going to be over – an end to her misery. But right now, she was beside herself with grief. He had always had an eye for other women. Veronica accepted his behaviour, because he said it was something that all men did, it was just the mechanics of being a man, almost like it was predestined.

"Who will want me now?" she asked. She had many qualities but she could not see them; her self-esteem had been stolen. She cried night and day when they separated, she would ring his phone just to hear his voice, her dignity abandoned. The pain was unbearable. She would beg him, "Please don't do this." She was desperate. She even suggested bringing another woman into their relationship to spice it up. This was an idea he had put to her on several occasions in the past, but the mere thought of it then had made her sick to her stomach, but now she was willing to go ahead if it meant they would be together.

"No, it's over Veronica. Leave me alone," he said confidently.

For six months she was in a depression, falling further and further each month, until there was nowhere else for her to go. That's when she came to the conclusion that she was going to have to deal with what had happened and, more importantly, she was going to have to accept it, because he had made his decision. Now the only thing for her to do was to start rebuilding her life. She was nervous. She went through her phone book and got in touch with old friends. She felt funny about doing so, because she didn't know how they would react after so long. But in fact they were glad to hear from her. She had stopped seeing them when she met Lionel.

Slowly but surely, she started doing things again. She even got a new job. She had come through her darkest moment. However, it was around this time he rang her, to say he wanted her back. He had split up with his girlfriend. He said it was because she wouldn't give him any space, but when Veronica pressed him he admitted his new girlfriend had finished with him when she found him cheating.

Veronica replied, "So she would not put up with your behaviour like I did. Is that why you want me back? I'm actually happy now Lionel. I have all my friends back and all my family, all the people I lost when I met you, and I have a new job, and I have finally met someone who treats me in a way I never thought I deserved to be treated, because of my experience with you. It's over Lionel," she whispered to him confidently. "I won't be coming back to you ever, it's over for good."

What we can perceive to be the worst thing that ever happened to us can actually end up being the best thing.

Sex

Sex, we can't live without it. We refuse to do that. We can be relentless in our pursuit of it. We go on holiday, just the lads, just the girls, what happens, we end up shagging someone. Never mind, we can add it to a long list of secrets. Anyway, they say what happens in Vegas stays in Vegas. I was under the influence at the time so it doesn't count, does it? It wasn't my fault, it was the booze that had sex with her, it had nothing to do with me. I was mortified when I found out all the things it had done with her. I'd never do that. In fact I threw up.

The morning after, to show my disgust a hundred per cent faithful me, the booze isn't when people have too much alcohol they are innocent it is the alcohol which is guilty. Everyone loses their mind for a bit of hot sex, don't they? We don't want that marital sex though, no what a turn off that can be, we can sleep straight through that, it's so boring. When we are trying to snare someone, we go at it like rabbits. The minute we're in a confirmed relationship it's, not tonight, I don't feel like it. Why can't you just hold me? Who are you kidding? When we first met you were doing cartwheels, now I'm only after one thing. Who tricked who here?

What about the sex we have when we dream about the person we really want in bed with us. Is that cheating? We all do it, we want that kinky sex, that's what we want. The only thing with that kind of sex is it's not sustainable. It can't last for ever. We have to be realistic about things and that's when you start thinking beyond sex and other things that matter to you, like can you talk to the person you're with? Can you spend quality time with them? Do you care about them? Love them? Before you know it, you're talking about marriage and you've put your slippers back on again.

Sex is great, but it isn't everything.

Skin deep

We were going on the works' night out. Lewis had been telling me how beautiful his woman Samantha was for a long time now, but this was the night I was actually going to meet her. Lewis himself looked like a prince, so I knew any lady he had chosen to be with had to be attractive. He said his lady was an older woman, but she was drop dead gorgeous, so when I saw her that's what I had expected to see, a strikingly beautiful woman. Instead, she was very plain, quite skinny and she had false teeth, although otherwise she was a nice person. I thought how could Lewis have described her how he did and with so much passion? That's when I thought we are all different and maybe my image of who I thought was attractive wouldn't have appealed to him either.

Years later, I met a girl and she told me she had mentioned to all of her friends how good looking I was and how funny I was and now they all wanted to meet me. I started to feel a little bit nervous about what she had said, because I had a flashback to Lewis telling me how stunning his fiancée was and I remembered thinking that she wasn't. I asked my girl not to say anything more to her friends until I had met them just in case they saw me and they thought I was ugly. She told me to stop being stupid. I thought about it, then I told her to say whatever she wanted. After all, it was how she felt about me that mattered, not what anyone else did – just like Lewis was mesmerised by his woman.

It's not a competition – choose the person who is right for you.

A good old domestic

My house

"I don't want you here. Have you heard me? Leeeave. Pack your bags and piss off. I don't want you here any more!" The tension was like a pressure cooker. Suddenly, the atmosphere would be too much and it would be round one all over again and the gloves would be off. Think of the most hurtful and despicable things you could say to someone – that's the rules we were playing by.

"You ruined my life."

"No, you ruined my life."

"I'm sick of your miserable attitude and face. Drop the key off on your way out."

"But where will I go?"

"I don't give a fuck where you go or who you go to as long as it's far from here. I'm not bothered."

"You fucking bitch! I gave my own place up for you."

"Well that's too bad and you can't keep using that look if you stay. I'm just going to start hating you. Go to your mum's, she will take you back."

"But I'm a grown man. Why do you want me to go every time we have a problem? Do you think this solves things? My mum has a right to her own life now she's raised her children. Look, I'll stay here, until I get a place of my own. Is that okay?"

"I don't think so. You're not using me until you find somewhere. I've told you, I want you gone out of this house, today preferably. Now if I have to start screaming, I will. Can't you see nothing's going to get better?"

"Is it over between us?"

"I don't know, but I can't do with you tonight, the way you twist and turn things, everything's always my fault you're so perfect."

"Look I'll stay on the sofa."

"No, I want you out. Just go will you, go, I need space to think. Go!"

"Who you talking to like that?"

"I'm talking to you."

"You think I'm a fucking yoyo! I'll fucking..."

"Yeah, you'll do what? Are you trying to scare me? C'mon, let's have it then. Give it ya best shot!

"You just dare. Fuck the fuck off! Go, now, there's the door."

This part of the programme is called the wind-up and it can lead to wrestling on the floor and trying to kill each other, but within a split second everything could change and we would be all right again. The walls where we lived were paper thin, so God knows what the neighbours thought of us. We'd see them sometimes in the morning, when we were on our way to work.

"Good morning."

"Good morning."

Hell knows what they thought of us. "Get out of my house!" That's what I was told, so I got my own house. When I got my own house, I was suddenly invited back into her house. It took me a while to realise, to really get it. I didn't have to go back and forth like this, day after day, because I had my own house...

Something's going on

I knew something was going on. I'd walk into a room and she would walk out. Or, she would be in a room and as soon as I came in, the whispering would start and suddenly she would put the phone down. She was getting dressed up all the time and she asked if she could borrow a little bit of money. I just thought, well, where's all your money gone? She said something had come up, a bill she had forgotten to pay, but when I had finished quizzing her about it, I didn't believe her. And, it was going to be my birthday on the Friday she said she had been called in to work. In over ten years, I can't remember a single time when she was called in to work and on a Friday night, too. She must think I'm a fucking idiot!

I played her at her own game. I walked into our house unexpectedly and said, "What are you doing here then? I thought you were supposed to be at work. What the fuck are you up to? What are you doing behind my back you lying bitch?" I had one hand around her throat, squeezing the life out of her and, all of a sudden, the light went on and everyone shouted "surprise surprise!" I couldn't believe it. She had planned a surprise birthday party for me and here I was screaming and choking her in front of a hundred guests! She had just been trying to show me a good time and I had ruined everything. I knew what I was doing but it was like I couldn't help myself. I let my suspicion and my imagination get the better of me. It's like once I got an idea in my head, it was set in stone.

But after that night, I don't react to every single thought I have any more because it can make a bad situation worse. If you think in a negative way, it can cause negative things to happen, and most of the time it was just me feeling insecure and reading too much into things.

You don't have to give into every emotion you have and you don't have to let paranoid thoughts come between you and your happiness. Think positively!

The big silence

We're back on the merry-go-round not talking again. We haven't spoken for a week now, still it's better than the last time – it was three months then. Zilch communication. Yes and no one-word answers, and don't forget the aggressive tone at the end of it. It's all your fault, if you... no it's your fault, if you... Some of the things we keep in our heads.

I wish I'd never met you. I can do better than you. I was happy before I met you. I fell for your crap. You were a different person then or should I say you was putting an act on you big fake. You made sure you turned up on time then. Etc, etc, etc.

Well, what about you? Sex wasn't a problem then was it darling? You were more than able then, now who's the fake? It takes one to know one and you weren't guzzling booze down your neck every night, so you've got room to talk. I should have stayed on my own. Etc, etc, etc.

These are the things that are unsaid so when there are no smiles and emptiness, this is what's going on between us. I'll ask you what's wrong and you'll say *nothing* and you'll ask me what's wrong and I'll say *nothing*. We don't want to say how we really feel or what has upset us, because if we do, we will be acknowledging we have a problem and it might make things worse and what could that lead to? Nobody wants that. No, better for us to stay silent. The only thing with staying silent, is that it can be worse than arguing. Tell you what, you don't speak to me I won't speak to you. Maybe we can drag it out for a few more weeks and our problems will sort themselves out all on their own.

Silence is not always golden.

Calendar days

I don't even know what there is to argue about. Even when there's nothing to argue about, we can make an argument out of something. We can seem to get on okay for a while, then we both end up waiting for something to go terribly wrong and when it happens it doesn't come with a huge announcement, it can just be something simple like a sharp reply to a question, or we are stewing about something that's happened at work. Instead of leaving it at work, we bring it home and before you know it swords are drawn and we are going in for the kill. This is usually when we refer to the calendar and pull out negative things about each other that have happened during our time together, hurtful things, the kind of things which are best left in the past, the things if we were getting on okay we would not speak of, such as:

"I know you did something with her. I remember when it happened, you couldn't even look me in the eye."

"I told you nothing happened... that was nineteen years ago."

"Yes, but it still cuts me to the core like it was yesterday."

"Well I didn't take that job because you said you wanted to finish off your studies. That job would have changed my life and then in the end you quit. You dropped out. I'll never forgive you for that."

"Now who's bringing up the past. You're just as bad as I am. That was ten years ago..."

Everyone has moments in the calendar. Times when they could have done things better, or things they are ashamed of, but if you're going to keep drawing from it and pulling out painful experiences every time you have an argument, how is that going to help?

Seeing Red

Big bully

Dear Gillian,

We work together side by side. We work for the same company and the same team. So why are things the way they are? Why have you taken an instant dislike to me and tried to make my life a living hell? Since the very first day I started, you've mocked me, disregarded my opinions, my ideas and any contributions I make. I am made to feel like what I say is not important, like I don't have a voice and I shouldn't say anything at all. What do you want from me? Why do you sabotage every single thing I do and belittle it? Why is that? I don't want your job. I'm comfortable where I am. I just want to do what I do, that's all. I'm not as popular as you, you know that. And I'm not as confident, and people don't like me, in the same way they like you. You have a powerful presence in the office, I can't compete with you. All I want to do is get through the day without any hassle.

I'm finding all of this really stressful now and there's no need for it. I'm sick of it. It's really beginning to affect my health. If this continues, I will be taking it higher, much higher. I need you to know this. I'm just asking for a chance to stay in the job I like, a chance not to have to feel nervous, not to feel inadequate, not to be worried about what I say in case it doesn't come out right, not to feel stupid, not to feel weak. Not to feel like I don't exist, not to feel any of those emotions. Is that too much to ask for? And Julia told me you've been poisoning everyone against me. Well, it's worked. I don't have any friends now. She also said it's not the first time you've behaved this way with someone – you've done it before.

What do you actually gain from this? How does it make your life any better? Just put yourself in my shoes for one minute. How would you like it if things were the other way around and you were being treated how you're treating me? Or, how about if it was a member of your family on the receiving end? If roles were reversed, do you think you would like it? I'm concerned about you even though you're trying to make my life a misery. I'm worried about you. I think something's happened to you in your past and you haven't been able to deal with it, so you vent your anger and frustrations out on other people and try to hurt them, instead of dealing with what's really going on inside your head. Can you tell me what happened? Were you bullied? Is that what this is all about? Listen, if you want to grab some time together and sit down and speak as two adults, I'd only be too happy to oblige, that's fine. Please do not hesitate to contact me. I am available to speak to you at any time and offer you any support you need.

Yours sincerely,

Janice

Dad

I know you hate gays, but please don't hurt my dad, he's the only family I've got. See, my mum walked out of my life when I was only three years old and dad raised me almost single-handedly. He says being gay wasn't a choice for him and that you either are or you're not, it's as simple as that. He's had a tough life raising me on his own, but he never once quit on me.

For the last fifteen years he's had to lead his life in secrecy, but I'm concerned now, because I think he's got to the point where he just doesn't care any more. He's sick of living a lie and not being true to himself. I know what happens to gays when they get sick of keeping their lives secret and decide to come out. People like you want to attack them, put bricks through their windows and smear graffiti all over their property and worse. Some of you even want to kill them. Well my dad is a good person.

He's lived his life for everyone else so far. Now, he wants to live it for himself. He deserves to be happy, so please don't hurt my dad. He's the only person who's been there for me, he's all I've got. Don't hurt my dad.

Self-preservation

Fifteen years I've worked for this law firm and out of nowhere she shows up. Okay, I wasn't exactly a hundred per cent honest about everything on my CV; about which University I went to and my training. But so what, I forged a few certificates, but look at what I've done since. I've more than proven myself over the years. I've become one of the most prominent and best lawyers in the whole country, and now there's a chance of her ruining everything for me, everything I've worked for and built up over the years.

My problem is she went to Cambridge. I said I went there too. If it comes out that I didn't, I'm finished. She's asked me on a few occasions questions about tutors and students who were there when I was there and I've struggled to know what to say. Questions about who I hung out with and what bars we went to... she just won't let it go. I've been so tense and so nervous about bumping into her again. Of all the firms she could have gone to, why did she have to get a job here?

I've tried avoiding her, tried not to attend the same meetings, but it's getting more and more difficult now, so I've come up with the only logical and rational thing I can think of. I didn't want to, but I'm going to have to kill her, aren't I? Well what else can I do? It's either that or I risk losing my job, the house, my lifestyle; my kids are at risk of losing their education, all the money I've put into their schooling. They don't deserve that do they? It's definitely not fair to hurt them, it's not right. Plus, I might even go to prison. So you see, I have no choice really, I'm backed into a corner.

I'm going to ask her if she fancies going for a drink one day after work. Then I'll spike her drink with Rohypnol. I've got some strong nylon rope. I'm going to tie it around her throat and just pull as hard as I can until she chokes and finally stops breathing. Then, I'm going to put her in the boot of my car. I've already dug the grave I'm going to put her in and I intend to be back in work the following day to represent my next client. I hate defending some of these scumbags. I'm going to be defending a man named Daniel Cliffe. He killed his uncle so he could claim the insurance money, shot him twice in the head at point blank range. The kinda people I have to work with, I tell you there are some real crazies out there!

Space

She wouldn't leave me alone. I mean, I wouldn't leave her alone. She was turning up everywhere I was, it was getting very scary. I mean, I was showing up at her work, her home, I was really beginning to freak her out. People around me started to get concerned for me. Her family had every right to be worried for her safety. The more and more I ignored her, the worse she got. I mean, I told her if she kept on ignoring me, she would regret it. She was following me everywhere, it was getting out of hand. By this time, I was watching her twenty-four hours a day nonstop. She'd had enough and she went to the police. I was arrested and locked up.

She kept on seeing him, deliberately winding me up I mean, so I broke in her flat and I trashed it. She was laughing at me, letting me know she could keep on doing it and getting away with it. I mean, no matter how hard they tried, the police couldn't stop me. So now everyone started to threaten me. So I made my mind up. I was going to kill the bitch. Then, she attacked me. I mean, I attacked her. She was going to leave me. All the turmoil and torture I was put through. Finally, I lost it and I killed her and now I have nobody.

See, when I met her she was all right, but after a bit she changed so quickly. She said she needed some space to herself, which I thought was nonsense. How can two people in love not want to share every single second together? She said I was suffocating her. She thought she could dismiss me like a pile of rubbish, and that jerk she took up with was rubbing my face in it. No, I'm glad she's dead. She was making my life unbearable.

On a happier note, I received some good news today. If I keep my nose clean and keep on doing what I'm doing, I'll be due for early release in 2019. That will be eight years I've spent in here, which really shouldn't have happened in the first place. It's unfair, but hopefully, once I'm out, I'll get the chance to rebuild my life, start from scratch again and, who knows, maybe next time around I'll end up meeting somebody decent.

Happy traveller

I had to slam my brakes on. My car was still skidding for a while before it stopped. I jumped out and ran straight over to his car. He was sitting there trying to lock his door, but I was too fast for him. He was saying he was sorry, but it was too late for that. It was like a red mist came over me and I blacked out. I started to swear at him.

"You daft twat!" I hit him as hard as I could. I was punching him in his face repeatedly. His blood was dripping down my fists. I got his arm, then I got the car door, and I was slamming it back and forth. He was screaming at me, begging me at the top of his voice to stop. I dragged him out of his motor and started jumping on him. He was a picture.

You might wonder what he did to me. He pulled out on me at a junction. I wasn't happy. It could have been a genuine mistake, an accident, but I didn't care, I swear I wanted him to die. Because of it, I forgot about all the times I'd pulled out on other people and the times when I'd given the wrong signals. I was the world's best driver and it was all about him and what he had done. I was swearing at him, calling his mum a slag. I wanted his blood for that fifteen minute period. I completely lost all sanity.

Truth is, I'd been arguing with the Mrs, all night, so I was in a foul mood that morning when I woke up. I was just asking for someone to piss me off, anybody, and unfortunately he just ended up being the poor soul on the receiving end. Now his life's changed for ever. He's going to need numerous operations, just to get some movement back in his arm. They say all his nerve ends were damaged. I'm not normally a violent person, but because of the nature of the offence they threw the book at me. I'm doing my porridge right now.

Something else the police told me that I didn't know, he had his five-year-old kid in the back of the car with him at the time. Apparently he hid under the back seat. Don't do what I did.

Get your rage under control before it ends up killing somebody.

No reason

"I fucking hate my man."

"Wait a minute, think about it rationally, why do you hate him?"

"It's just the way he walks."

"So you hate him because of how he walks?"

"Not just that, because he thinks he's better than everyone else."

"Has he said that to you?"

"No, but that's the way he is. I feel like crushing his head. He thinks he's better than everyone, because he's been to University."

"Is that what all this is about? You could go to University. There's nothing stopping you "He has an attitude, he's ignorant."

"So wait, have you ever been introduced?"

"No."

"Have you ever spoken to each other?"

"No."

"So how can you really know what he's like?"

"Look just leave me alone, I just don't fucking like him. Get off my back."

We should question what it is about us that makes us behave the way we do rather than point the finger at others.

Raquel

I told Raquel a thousand times to clean her room out. She shut the door in my face and told me to get lost. I could have swung for her, but I never did. She was always bunking off school. We were always getting the phone calls from her teachers, and I caught her smoking in her room one day when I came home early from work – thirteen years old, can you believe it? I had already told her I didn't approve. "Look at me when I'm talking to you!" She just used to look up at the ceiling, chewing her gum.

Her mum couldn't cope with her either. She was making both of our lives a misery. She wouldn't even wash a cup out. She was always hanging out in the park, drinking and coming home late at night.

I was the one in full-time work. I was the one paying the bills to keep the roof over our heads, but no one takes that into consideration now do they? The amount of hours I was putting in a week down at that factory, to make sure we were on top of everything and that we were able to afford some of the small luxuries in life, like being able to take a trip down to Butlins or up to Blackpool for a few days at a time. But no, she didn't appreciate any of that. I might as well not have bothered. I just wanted her to have a bit of respect and at least recognise what I had done for her, instead of always harping on about her dad.

I mean, just where was her real dad? What was his contribution? She never even got a postcard from him, but yet she talked about him like he was a saint when I was the one who was raising her, bringing her up. And, to tell the truth, I was a bit disappointed with Elsie too, for letting Raquel keep a picture of her dad up in her room. I didn't like it one bit. Why did he deserve that? If you ask me, he was a first class bastard.

I tried to tell Elsie she was with me now. I was her partner and Raquel's step-father and all that they had with *him* was in the past and that's where it should stay. I'd brought Raquel up and he'd never paid her any mind, so why should he have his picture up on my walls? Elsie would answer back and say, "It's her Dad. She can have his picture up if she wants." I mean, where was the support she could have given me? There was none. Anyway, I'm only human. Years of talking back to me and saying I couldn't tell her what to do, I wasn't her dad, and eventually I snapped and hit her. It was the first time, though everyone was quick to forget all the good things I'd done for them. I was a bit heavy handed I admit. I broke her nose in three places. But everyone makes mistakes. We come to accept that as being part of life, so why my mistakes should be blown up out of all proportion I have no idea. I've had to pay the price for that and they say child abuse is child abuse, but look at all the pressure I was under. Surely all these cases shouldn't be tarred with the same brush – but looked at under their own set of individual circumstances, which would be a much fairer system.

I'm not mad any more, anyway. I've got over it. As they say, "time to move on". One good thing to come out of this is that Elsie and I have patched things up. We're still a bit worried about Raquel though because she's drinking double the amount she used to be.

Denial is denial but abuse will always be abuse.

Vigilantes

Jeff: I told him if he ever put his hands on her again, I'd finish him. I warned him, he's got no more chances this time, this is it.

Andy: What do you mean?

Jeff: I mean he's a corpse, he's a dead man. I'm going to get my gun and I'm going to kill him! What would you do if it was your sister?

Andy: I'd cut his nuts off!

Jeff: Are you coming, Andy?

Andy: Try and stop me, I'm in a hundred per cent.

We went to his house and we killed him. We fired three shots into his chest for what he did to his sister. Jeff said he had it coming to him. I was arrested. I've only got two life sentences to serve. I'm never getting out of here. It wasn't just him that died that night. I should never have been there, my life's finished too.

Alternative ending...

Jeff: Andy, are you coming?

Andy: No, look just get the police involved. I'm not down for all this vigilante stuff. I've got a wife and family at home. I'm sorry about what happened to your sister, Jeff, but killing him isn't going to bring her back. I can't go with you, I'm sorry. I don't think you should go either.

Jeff: Oh well fuck off then. All the favours I've done for you over the years.

Andy: I'm sorry Jeff.

Andy didn't like letting his best friend down, but he told him he couldn't get involved in killing anyone. That is why Andy is a free man today and Jeff is rotting away in prison. And Andy was right, it didn't bring his sister back.

Before you get involved in something that could get you locked up for ever, think about it, because you probably won't ever see the light of day again. Just like Jeff, many people do things in the heat of the moment, then have the rest of their lives to think about it from a dark rusty cold decrepit jail cell.

In the system

Jailhouse

I spent the last thirteen years in and out of prison. The most I spent on the outside was ten months and I was straight back in for armed robbery, and possession of a firearm. That was a bitch, but I know my life's gonna be different. I've had time to think. I know what's important to me now. I can't spend my whole life on lockdown, so when I'm released in six months, I'm going to run my programme different. I ain't ever coming back to this cage. I'm gonna try get an education and be somebody. I don't wanna be a gangsta, dats not where I wanna be at. I've spent too long in the jailhouse and what about my gyal and my yout? She stood by me. Every visit she's been dere. She told me all she wants me to do is be dere for her and Jamal and that he needs a dad in his life, a role model, not someone who's going in and out of prison. The last time she came here I told her I was gonna marry her, as soon as I get out so we can be together. I swear she cried. Well we both did, but that don't make me no pussy though. She said she had been waiting for ever for me to mutter those words. I'm going to ask her again when I'm on the outside, and do it proper and get her the baddest ring, she deserves dat.

My friends, I don't see any of dem, where are dey now? Dem man stepped the fuck off and I haven't heard shit from them, not even one letter. I can't come back here, I can't let Sophie down or my family. Nah b more dan dat,

I can't let myself down, when I'm back on the outside. I'm going places. I ain't moving with none of those guys any more like Stickup Man and Tubbsy. When I hang around with dem, we act the fool, get into trouble with other crews and five o', I start drinking. I don't think and I end up doing dumb shit. Me and my gyal and little Jamal are going to be a proper family. He's almost ten now my six months is up.

The Day of Release

I feel great. This is the moment I was waiting for. I told the screws I was never coming back and I'd send 'em a postcard. I got my belongings and I was outta dere. I got a taxi back down to the manor, saw my Sophie. She looked so good. It was nice to be home with her and my son. It was a blessing and a new start for me.

First few weeks, I stayed away from certain man, but it's hard cos dem guys are all I knew and I couldn't be around Sophie 24/7 could I? I'd been trying to get some work, I really had, but I was getting nowhere. As soon as they heard about my criminal record, the doors just closed one after another. I was fed up and frustrated. Sophie asked me to hang in there until something came up. She asked if I could be patient. I told her I could, but I had no idea it would be this hard. So when Stickup Man and Tubbsy belled me and ask me if I wanted to come round and play some cards and get a drink, they were gonna watch the new Denzel movie, I said "Okay".

Well we got smashed up, den we went out on da road. We were just cruising, windows low, music bumping, and Tubbsy said he knew dis house up Fixby where we could make a raise. Fixby is a rich man's end. People up dere are minted. If you live up there, you know you done good. He said we could get some serious money and that he had done da homework. He had been checkin this place out for the last three months. Dats when he said he had a shotgun in the boot of the car, but it probably wouldn't have to come to that.

We had drunk three bottles of vodka and been slurping on the brandy. I said no at first then they laughed and asked me how I was making ends meet on my benefits and something snapped. I forgot about my gyal Sophie and Jamal and I thought, *they're right, I need some funds. I can't survive on £140 a fortnight!*

So I told them, "I'm in!"

We went to the house Tubbsy mentioned. He was right; no one was in, just like he said. We took everything out of that bitch, emptied it out; laptops, phones, credit cards, jewellery, the lot. Only I cut my hand on the way out the window. I didn't even feel the cut, but my DNA was all over the place. That's how I got back in here and I don't understand it. The screws just laughed at me and said, "Welcome back home!" I was only on the outside for three months. I don't understand how I got back in here. It's quite simple. You did the same shit that got you in here the last time you were here.

If you don't change, nothing will!

Street life

I wanted to let them know how hard I was and I wasn't to be messed with. If they even looked at me sideways, I didn't care who it was I'd ask them if they had a problem. If they paused I would explode on them. I was the main man on the street. My clique was untouchable, I was very important. If I went to a restaurant, I would leave a tip of about £100 for the waiter so anyone who was around could see I had money in abundance.

Other times, I wasn't such a nice guy and I'd tell the waiter to bring me another meal and look sharp about it cos I wasn't happy with what was on my plate. I'd tell 'em it wasn't good enough and if they weren't quick about it, I'd cause a scene and kick off big time. My lady loved to see all the power I had and sometimes I'd put my hand up her dress whilst I was waiting for the food to arrive. It turned her on. I just did it, ha-ha, I didn't care who was there. I was nasty like dat ruthless. I had my blade and gun with me so I was set. That was how I used to be.

Everything was going okay until I had some beef with this guy called Soldier. Because he was acting like he was the man, I had to run my knife across his face to show him who really was. That's why they came for me. I was coming out of Patel's near the bookies' on Shears Avenue when this Beamer pulled up alongside me. The window went down and they just started firing shots. I was hit once in my back and twice in my leg.

I was taken to Dunfields Hospital. They told me they were going to have to amputate my leg, that they couldn't save it. Whoa, that was difficult for me to hear. My head was wrecked; I was all alone. And the visits from my gang were few and far between. In the end they stopped coming full stop. Even my girl, Trish, who had been wid me since the beginning, bailed on me and she told me when I used to touch her up at the restaurant, she hated it and she found it disgusting. She said I behaved like a complete prick. She also said she'd wanted to leave me years ago, but was just too afraid to do so, but she wasn't any more and she walked out of my life for good that day.

That was a turning point for me. I looked at my life for real and made drastic changes cos when I think about it, it was no life at all. I had been a first class chief and I lost my leg because of it. Partly cos I wanted to be accepted and have respect out on the streets. I even thought of those guys as my family. What a fool I was. When the chips were down they were nowhere to be seen, in fact I had to keep one eye on them as much as I did my enemies, so that line they spin about family really is just a line. Since then, I've learned what real respect is.

Nowadays, I don't have the flashy cars any more nor the swagger or attitude I used to have, but what I do have is much better, because I've got peace of mind now. Because I'm finally being me. In a way, it took a bullet for me to change my life and that same bullet could have ended it. But you might not be so lucky!

Betrayed

He did not intend the situation to turn out how it did. It's true, they had bad blood between them, and there had been an ongoing feud for the last year or so, but no one could have predicted how it would eventually go down. He had originally bought the knife just for protection, so his enemy could see he was prepared to defend himself. That was all. He was not prepared to use it, but when his younger brother was beaten up, by the same gang, on his way home from school, that's what did it.

Mark was just a fifteen-year-old innocent schoolboy. The beating his brother took incensed him. He wasn't part of their lifestyle. He'd had nothing to do with the world of drugs, so why get him involved? Why pick on him? No, this time Luke Richards had gone too far. Jake wanted to scare him, make him know he had to leave him and his family alone, he had crossed a line. So he went to his house one night and, just to make the threat more serious, he had brought a gun too. He was just going to frighten him.

He had been watching the house for a couple of nights, his cousin and his best friend keeping a look-out for him to make sure there was no one passing by. It was pitch black. He put his mask and gloves on, entered through Luke's back window and crept up the stairwell, gun fully exposed. He thought about what had been done to his brother. *Why get him involved?* He said to himself again. *You wanna fuck with me? My family? You wanna die?*

There was a scuffle and a fight took place. Luke and Jake were wrestling on the floor for a minute or so, then the gun went off on its own and shot Luke five times in his chest. He was dead. Then the knife jumped out of Jake's jacket and, just to make sure, it stabbed Luke as well. Both the gun and knife had betrayed Jake that night. He had just wanted to scare Luke because of what he had done to his brother, but in the midst of all the action the gun and knife got excited and decided they wanted to get involved. He didn't want to kill him, but his weapons had minds of their own.

If you're carrying a blade or a gun how do you know they won't betray you? The best way of making sure is not to carry them in the first place. Because then, you can't use them, you won't have to live the rest of your days locked up in prison, and, most importantly of all, no one has to die.

Beyond the grave

Addicted

I used to be one for going out. I had a good job and was really into my fashion. I had the snappiest clothes. I loved going out with my mates clubbing. We used to go down to Bolton, Liverpool, Warrington, meeting people; well, meeting ladies to be precise, all over the place, practising our chat-up lines. I know it sounds childish now, but everyone's young at least once in their lives, aren't they? And we had a good time seeing who could pull the most birds. It was all young boys' stuff, I admit, but I was happy. Back then, I didn't have a care in the world.

I bumped into Ricky Andrews. That's what happened. I had known him since I was seven years old. That's how far we went back. I saw him on Ridley Road one day and we just got talking. He was a great guy, Ricky, and even though I'd not seen him for years we still got on the same as we used to. He invited me to his home, said he had some friends calling round and he'd like it if I came along. They were gonna get some records out, play some music and smoke a joint. To tell the truth, it didn't sound that exciting to me, sitting indoors on a Saturday night, but I liked Ricky so I went around.

The lights were dimmed and everyone was sat in a circle either building a spliff or passing a spliff. Part of me thought, *how sad is this? This isn't living, sat indoors getting doped up on a Saturday night. The best night of the week, what are these guys doing?* But I was there now. Ricky passed me a spliff and said, "Try this mate." I thought about saying no, but I didn't wanna seem uncool, so I took it. I had a few pulls. I didn't even like it really. I stayed for about an hour then left. He told me to come around again and I don't know why but a few days later I called back. I tried some more weed.

This time, it didn't make me feel as bad as the first time and everyone was laughing. It was a good atmosphere. Danny and Simon had the giggles and Ray and Ricky were having their own conversation, talking about philosophy, I think. I thought to myself, these people are okay. After that, I started going to Ricky's pretty regularly, only trying other things, Es, Acid, Magic Mushrooms, Speed, Cocaine – we were doing everything.

After a bit, I was the same as everyone else. I stopped going out, I stopped spending money on clothes, I stopped being bothered about my appearance and I even stopped going to work. Too tired from being smashed up the night before I was ringing in sick all the time until eventually they sacked me. I just took more drugs to dull the pain – it became the answer for everything. That's when I found out Ricky's mates weren't so cool after all and that without the drugs they were different people. We were onto the proper hard gear by then. Everything had spiralled out of control. Now it wasn't a choice of if we needed the drugs, but more like we had to take them just to feel normal.

Some of the gang were stealing, doing burglaries, shoplifting, nicking cars and nicking lead to pay for their habit. I had more respect for myself. I wasn't one of those addicts – apart from those times which nobody knows about, like when my mum's wedding ring went missing or some money disappeared from my brother's account. Apart from those times, I swear on a stack of Bibles, I'd never do anything like that. Times changed and I moved on. I stopped hanging around with Ricky, Ray and the rest of 'em. They weren't for me, but I was still using, I still had problems. I got so low, I even had to go to a drugs agency to get help. My family were worried about me. They thought I was having a nervous breakdown. I was having headaches, panic attacks and I was hardly sleeping.

One day when I was out, I bumped into Carlos and Theo, some of my old clubbing mates from my life before drugs. I was so humiliated. I tried to walk straight past them only Carlos recognised me. I reeked of sweat. I'd not had a bath for weeks. They had nice girls with them and nice cars. They said they were glad to see me, but I could tell they were totally embarrassed. That was a bad time for me. I decided to knock the drugs on the head and I did. I was actually clean for about eighteen months. But one thing you've got to know is that even if you're not using drugs or drink or whatever it is you're addicted to, it stays upstairs in your head, it's always on your mind, so you can't afford to dabble. I thought I could. I see my nephew, Mason, and he's following the same path I did and I wanna tell him to get a grip, tell him he doesn't need drugs to live his life. But, I can't because that's how I ended mine. I'd just made a plan to quit again for the seventh or eighth time and I was serious about it, I really was, but I thought *just one last time*. And it really was. I overdosed and died. You always think it happens to someone else. I had a lot of opportunities to quit but I never did.

I had a fantastic eulogy at my funeral. They said I had a promising career in engineering and had it not been for my tragic involvement in drugs twelve years ago, I could have been anything I wanted. Yes, I remember my life before drugs. I could have done anything, but once the drugs take hold of you, it's not that easy and I can't turn the clock back now. If only I'd felt like this when I was alive.

Some experiments just aren't worth experimenting with.

No secret worth keeping

You knew who murdered me and you didn't say a thing. You kept it to yourself. You coulda said something and you didn't. You didn't say a word. My mum had to suffer every single day not knowing where I was. I went down as a missing person and I'm still missing now. You see my killer and you think it's okay for him to do what he did to me and get away with it. I was stabbed seventeen times and what for? Because I asked a lady for a dance on a night out on the town. Because of that, your psycho brother followed me on my way home and killed me. How was I to know she was his ex-girlfriend? It was just a dance I asked for. I'm cold, I'm still out here.

My case is still open, my family can't even have a burial, a funeral to lay me to rest. I don't know if you know what it's like to see your own mum and dad suffering. They're not living life any more, it's ripped them to shreds. You're just as bad as the person who did this to me, because you think it's okay, you condoned it, you talked yourself out of going to the police by saying, "Well, what good would it do? He's already dead now, it would just ruin another life" – i.e. your brother's life.

You also got yourself off the hook by saying that you're not a grass. *Hello*, pardon me, *we're talking about a bloody murder over here*. Well I had a family too. A seven-year-old daughter. She's real. She's called Jessie and she was the apple of my eye and I'm never going to see her again. I know it may be hard for you, but he doesn't deserve to be free. Suppose he does it again? Do you really want that on your conscience? Please pick up a phone or go to the station, tell 'em where I'm buried and let my family have some peace again.

There's loads of unsolved murders, people like me lying in gutters, under floorboards and at the bottom of a river, because people that knew something stayed quiet. Some secrets shouldn't be kept, that's the truth of it. Do the right thing. All I wanna do is get off the missing persons' list and go home to my family, so they can finally have some closure. Is that too much to ask for?

The afterlife

John O'Neil was cycling to work on Friday morning, as he did every Friday morning, when his bike was hit by a lorry. The driver of the lorry did not see him as he was in his blind spot. They say he died instantly, but what's weird about this story is that witnesses testify to seeing John later on inside a café just near the scene of the accident. The big, friendly Irish guy with the magnetic smile and warm heart. They all remembered him.

That day he apparently spoke to everyone, but yet he was thought to have been killed instantly. So what does that tell us? Is there life after death? Was John really dead? His body was certainly still sprawled out in the street. When ambulances arrived, he was pronounced dead. They say in all likelihood he would have died the moment the lorry collided with his bicycle, but yet witnesses say he was in the cafeteria for at least thirty minutes after his death.

Those who study reincarnation say it wasn't an apparition that the people saw at the café, but that it was John and he had passed over to the afterlife.

We only believe in what we know but there is so much that we do not know.

Keep smiling John O Neil!

Your very good health

Ready or not

When illness shows up on your doorstep, it doesn't ask if you're ready. Is this a good time for you? Is it convenient? Should It call back later, maybe in a few months or a few years when you're not so busy? Frankly it doesn't matter if you're busy or not or what your circumstances are. Full stop. Its sole purpose is to turn you upside down and hit you for six, that's it. You could be going through one of the best periods of your life. It just suddenly comes out of nowhere and tries to take you under. Something within us either starts working against us or stops protecting us. Loved ones watch helplessly from the side-lines as their lives are also torn in half, but there's nothing they can do, that is apart from pray, pray that things will get better and there will be an end to the suffering and those in pain will recover.

How much does someone's determination and willpower come into play in these situations? They say a positive mental attitude can be a lifesaver. Up and down on an emotional roller coaster, pulled and dragged in every direction possible, and this is only the beginning. The tears flow deeper and more intensely than any river known to us, from everyone involved. People say why me, why you, why anybody? We don't know why, 'just because' is why. It's a mystery we need to make sense of.

Doctors are baffled; second opinions, third opinions and other experts scratch their heads and offer their diagnoses. To what extent has the illness progressed and how serious is it? Has the person's life changed for ever? Will they ever be the same again? Or worse, is this the end? Should we be making plans, finalising everything, bringing one's house into order, as it were?

Why it is some people become ill and others do not when they tend to have little regard for their health? We do not know the answer to that question either. What we do know is when illness does come knocking, we hope it will not be of the fierce kind but one that we are able to overcome so we are able to start rebuilding our lives and we are able to offer everyone our upmost gratitude for the support they offered in our time of suffering and despair.

Do what you can to look after your health, because ill health could be closer than you think.

Make that appointment

Moirai Lang kept putting off going to see her doctor for a check-up for something that could be serious. She just wouldn't do it. Her brother asked her, her mum asked her, "Why won't you go Moirai?"

"Because I feel perfectly fine, there isn't a thing wrong with me. Now stop fussing."

Her toenail was black and her toes now had a strange greeny colour to them. In the end, she told her mother she would go, to stop her from whingeing and to shut her up. But she didn't go. Then, when her sisters asked her too, she would come up with excuses, reasons why she couldn't go: "I can't because I have to clean the floors in my house. I need to take my kitten for a walk. I have to finish weaving the cardigan I am making." She just wanted to be left to her own devices. She was sick of being pestered by everyone. She found the whole thing quite annoying.

In the end, the strange greeny colour travelled up both of her legs and by the time she got round to going to her doctor they were planning her funeral. She had been told she had six months to live. She had a simple illness which was left untreated and developed into something serious and she died of blood poisoning.

If you have a concern something doesn't look or feel right, don't ignore it. Don't take a chance, go to your doctor immediately. It could be the difference between life and death.

Raw

You first recognised you felt ill in 2005 after countless visits to the doctor. That is the same year your worst fears were confirmed. You have had this illness for ten years now. You don't have anyone you can confide in. In fact, you haven't confided in anyone at all. They say a problem shared is a problem halved but this is a secret which has remained with you. This is an illness nobody wants to readily admit to. It's a very personal illness. This is your own unique story of how it happened.

You were living in London in 2001 when you met Ben. He was introduced to you by a mutual friend. He was charming and very easy to get along with and you hit it off straight away. He had been doing missionary work in Africa for three years and had only been back in the UK for six months.

When you met, there was an instant attraction and you started seeing each other. Things started to progress between yourselves and you inevitably started to have a sexual relationship. You were apprehensive about this at first as no precautions were used but Ben assured you everything would be fine. Twelve months into the relationship, it was revealed to you that Ben was seeing another woman and that he was a compulsive liar. Without hesitation, you ended the relationship and thought nothing more of it.

Another twenty-four months later you started to feel strange sensations and felt unwell in general. You made an appointment to see your doctor. A few appointments more and that's when it was confirmed you had HIV, the illness which eventually develops into Aids. You tried desperately to contact Ben and finally, when you did, he put the phone down on you when you were in the middle of breaking the news to him. That's when you realised he had known all along. Since then, it's been a nightmare, torturing yourself over and over again with the same questions: *Why me, why didn't I protect myself?* You wanted to use something but Ben said it wasn't necessary. You wanted to say to him at the time you thought it was too risky, didn't you? Neither of you knew each other's sexual history, but in the heat of the moment you put it to the back of your mind and you had sex with him. Now look what's happened. It's the one thing you regret the most because of the devastating effect it's had on your life; constantly taking different tablets to try to suppress the virus. The white cells in your body which fight infection have all but collapsed. There's no resistance any more and what hurts even more than the pain is knowing that it could have all been prevented if only you had done what your instinct told you to do, if only you had used protection, if only you had insisted on using a condom. Well, all of this could have really been avoided, couldn't it?

If you're not using a contraceptive you're hoping you will be lucky that you won't catch a sexually transmitted disease, that there won't be a pregnancy or you won't get HIV. You don't have to hope if you use protection.

Worried

Joseph ran into the Royal Hertfordshire Hospital at top speed, down the corridor, faster than Usain Bolt. He knocked over two patients when he made his mad dash. He jumped to the front of the queue ahead of other people who were already in line. His shoulder was hanging out of his shirt, his arm uncovered.

"Check me now, this is an emergency, a matter of life and death! Check me now for God's sake! Will someone take my blood pressure? I'm about to have a stroke." One of the nurses ran towards him and at pace, stethoscope in hand. She took his blood pressure. It was 120/80.

He said, "Now tell me what it really is. I need to know."

"I have." She repeated it again. He didn't believe her at first, but she assured him she was telling him the truth. He had felt a stroke was imminent, but he left the hospital, his mind at ease.

Only a couple of days later, he went to his GP surgery. This time, he ran like a bull chasing a matador, almost smashing the double doors of the surgery as he crashed into them. He was banging on his chest in the entrance with no shirt on. It looked like it was a retake of one of those King Kong movies. "Help me, I'm about to have a heart attack. Help!" Two nurses came running to see what the matter was. They took his blood pressure, but everything was as it should be. It was normal. They gave him the results and he left with a big weight removed from his shoulders.

He bumped into one of his friends, Jarvis, he did from time to time, and asked him if he was okay. Jarvis replied, "Why?" He said he was concerned about him, because he looked dehydrated. Jarvis told him he had just had some water and he was fine. Joseph said, "Aren't you worried about your kidneys, if they are functioning okay?" Jarvis said, "No, not at all. A little bit of worrying is natural and can be positive, but you've been worrying for years. Every time I bump into you, about everything under the sun, Joseph, and what has it actually changed? There's nothing wrong with my kidneys or yours, my or your heart or anything else. It can't be good for you."

Joseph – "Hey, how so?"

Jarvis – "Well, all the worrying you've done, has it changed anything at all? Can you think of one positive thing to come out of it?"

Joseph – "Well, no."

Jarvis – "You've had your medicals and been told there's nothing wrong, but you won't accept it."

Joseph – "I know."

If something's going to happen, thinking about it every minute of every waking day won't change it. If all you're doing all day is worrying, try to put whatever you're worried about into context, because soon you might not have anything to worry about ever. Stress is a silent killer.

Families

Everything the child wants

I started buying gifts at the beginning of November. I bought our Ellie, who is two years old, a baby doll in a bath, a baby doll on a bike, a Peppa Pig caravan and play house, a Wendy house, a rocking horse, a bicycle and the most beautiful pram you've ever seen. Also a white carriage for her dolls to go in, a Dora the Explorer table and chair set, and a craft set, and a whole bunch of new clothes. I thought I'd make it really special for her. She was one year old on her first Christmas, so she couldn't really understand the concept of what it was all about, but she's two now, so she can now appreciate it.

She was looking forward to seeing Santa, so I just got her absolutely everything. And I bought our Cassie the latest mobile phone. I had to, she said, she was the only one in her class who didn't have one, and all the accessories too. I didn't want her to feel like she was missing out. She's as good as anybody at that school. I also bought her a tablet, a laptop, an MP4 player, a digital camera, some Versace perfume, a One Direction book set, and loads and loads and loads of dressing-up outfits, so she could dress as anything from a princess to Cinderella to Snow White. She said it was important, she needed them.

It's all over now and I've got a splitting headache. My whole left side of my face is hurting. I'm in a mess. I don't have anything for next month's bills. I think I got caught up in the excitement of it all. I wish I had really thought about what I was doing. I took a loan out. I went to The Money Shop, I borrowed quite a bit from them and I've run up three credit cards which I'm totally maxed out on, and the electricity and gas are running low. I didn't do a full food shop either, so I've hardly got any shopping in. I'll have to ask my friend Trudie for some money. I hope she has some otherwise I'm stuffed. I did it for the kids, so they would feel special, I didn't want that posh arse Vicky up the street looking down her nose at us, bragging about all the things she had bought her kids, so I spoiled them.

I can do it. I'll find the money from somewhere, I've done it before. You can't disappoint a child on Xmas Day, can you?

My parents used to say no to me. If the gifts I wanted were too expensive, they would say they couldn't afford them and ask me to choose something cheaper. But you can't say no to them these days, when all their friends have everything, can you? And you should have seen how excited they were when they were opening up their presents. Oh to see the smiles on their little faces. Well it is just priceless really.

Live today, pay tomorrow!

A balancing act

When Anna's daughter Phoebe passed her degree in English literature, she threw a massive party to mark the event. When Maria, her younger daughter, got the same distinction in the same subject a few months later, Anna hardly looked at her. She didn't make a fuss, she just said congratulations and carried on washing the dishes. Maria had done well in geography and biology too. This went unnoticed, but when her beloved Phoebe passed her driving test on the third time of asking, Anna shared the news with everyone. "My daughter has just passed her driving test. I tell you, look out for her, she's going places." This was appalling considering when Maria passed on her first attempt, her mum put it down to good luck and told her it was well known first-time drivers were not as accomplished as those who had taken the test again and she carried on reading her newspaper.

This had been a pattern of behaviour for years. Maria often felt she was not good enough to deserve her mum's love and attention, but she didn't know why. Things changed though when Anna took ill with pneumonia and needed to be looked after, because it was Maria that came to her side. Phoebe said she was far too busy to attend. She had a new boyfriend so her time was accounted for. She hoped her mum would understand. Maria stayed with her day and night until she was well again and her mum kissed her head and told her she had not behaved towards her in a way a mother should and she was ashamed. Maria rushed to her defence and said it wasn't true, but Anna said it was and asked her not to interrupt. "You are truly my angel. I felt Phoebe needed my attention, I have always been worried about her. I did everything I could to encourage anything she did and at the same time I overlooked all your achievements. It was wrong of me. I know Phoebe is spoilt and it's mostly my doing. I want things to be different between us in the future. Thank you for being here for me Maria." And she kissed her head again.

Anna looked deep within herself to find out what it was that had made her treat her two children so differently. It turned out it was Maria's father who Anna had held a grudge against, because of how he had been with her in their relationship; because Maria was a product of him, she had reacted to her in ways she was less than proud of. But she had seen the error of her ways. She also realised she had regarded Phoebe in a more favourable light because her dad had been her greatest love. Anna swore to change things and be a good mother to both of her children in the future and she did.

Love your children equally. That's fair, isn't it?

Sweet Abbi

Scott: And the winner of the Carer of the Year Award goes to Michael Lord. Michael, can you please come up to centre stage? *(Riotous applause)* What is it, Michael, that's made you work so hard this year? Not to say you don't work hard every year, ha-ha, no but this has truly been a defining moment in your career, where you have really excelled in all aspects of your work.

Michael: Well, to tell the truth Scott, the birth of my daughter Abbi really motivated me to do better and focus more, and the support from my good wife. I know it's not really the place to get sentimental, at an event like this, but if no one minds I'd like to read a few words I wrote about Abbi who has truly been an inspiration for me. Is that okay?

(Clap clap)

Sweet Abbi, so young, so vibrant, so mature, so outspoken and yet you are only two years of age. You are all I could imagine you could be. You have brought nothing but joy to my life. It was touch and go for a while, when your mother was in labour with you, and at one point we thought we had lost you. Fortunately, it was not to be. I thank God for being merciful and sparing your life. Just thinking of you can bring a smile to my face. How you enjoy life and seem to take everything you do in your stride. I love your spirit, your enthusiasm and determination to learn and figure things out for yourself and your curiosity and your stubbornness too. I saw your frustration when you tried to put your socks on and you couldn't quite do it. And I saw how it then turned to tears and yet when I offered to help you, you shouted "no" ever so sternly. That trait to fight for your own independence has revealed itself in other situations. Like when you were learning to put your coat on, you had to do it yourself or not at all, and at meal times when you insisted on feeding yourself, and even when we went to the park you wanted to go on the rides and slides alone without any help. But another thing that has always been apparent is your soft, caring nature, the hugs and cuddles you like giving, as well as receiving, and your adorable smile. I never thought I'd have an opportunity to be a father again. I am so happy and I am ever so proud of you, sweet Abbi. I know I have picked up this award today because of you. Thank you everyone.

(Clap clap)

Sweet Morgan

In my acceptance speech for that award the other week I said my inspiration over the last twelve months at work had been Abbi, and yet *you* were in the audience. You're my first daughter and I didn't acknowledge you, which was wrong. You are fifteen years old and Abbi only two.

Looking back, I realise I didn't give enough thought as to how you would feel. On the surface, it may appear that I have more love for her than I do for you, but nothing could be further from the truth. You are both my daughters and I love you equally. The simple fact is that I wasn't a great father to you. Your mother and I were continually battling and unfortunately the inevitable happened and we split up when you were just a tot.

That's when I went wrong. Instead of putting my time into you, I put it into me. I was trying to find my feet and find love, I was in a lot of pain and I put other women before seeing you and just other things in general. That's the honest truth and before I even realised ten years had disappeared that could have been ten years of getting to know you. Instead, I floated in and out of your life. I put my hands in the air. My own self-gratifying thirst is what got in the way of us becoming closer. I didn't want to be pinned down. I was searching for something to fix me. I felt all on my own. The ironic thing is that you could have taken away that loneliness. I didn't need someone else to fill that part of the jigsaw. I thought I did, but I didn't.

Now you are grown and that time has passed. I can smile though because you have turned into a lovely woman, all be it with not much help from me. Your grandma played a major part in your upbringing. In a way, she was the dad you never had. I should have been there for you, I wasn't. But I have learned from my mistakes and I'm trying to right my wrongs. I'm trying to do things better this time around, not because Abbi means more to me than you, but because I am in a better place now and I understand I might be in danger of repeating my actions all over again.

I understand it must be difficult for you to see me doing things with her that I never ever did with you and I accept it may take a while for us to work things out between us properly, but I'm willing to try because it's important to me. To do so, I've changed as a person. I know it's a bit late in the day and I've missed out on plenty, but all I am asking is for you to give me a chance to be a dad to you and for us to start from the beginning again. You are special to me, you're my big daughter, and no one, no person or thing, can take those feelings away. I love you, Sweet Morgan.

Is it ever too late to try to build a relationship with your child?

Nine months

Nine months it took me to get here. On two occasions, I almost didn't make it. And now that I am here, these two act like I'm an inconvenience to them. I can't believe it, they hate each other. All they ever do is argue and I feel that I'm to blame, because I know they never used to be as bad as this. I used to listen to them, when I was in Mummy's tummy. They used to laugh every now and then. Don't get me wrong, it wasn't perfect, but it's a whole lot worse now. I thought the drugs and everything would have stopped, but I guess things haven't turned out how they planned. Instead of bringing them closer, I've pulled them wide apart. Something's not right. All they ever do is get smashed, leave their bottles and stuff all over the place, syringes all over the place, and yesterday I had to sit in my shitty nappy nearly all day.

I cried and I screamed as loud as I could to get Mum's attention – that's my way of trying to tell her something's not right. She just told me to be quiet, to shut the fuck up! She was sick of hearing it and if I didn't shut up soon she'd really give me something to cry about. I had to whimper, take deep breaths and try and hold it in. I was in a right state, shaking with fear because at that moment she looked totally insane.

I didn't know what she was going to do. She looked so unstable. I think it's because she didn't have any cigarettes or drink. It wasn't her fault, she didn't have anything to calm her down, I don't want to get smacked again, the last time I was sore for ages. What was it now? Oh yes, I remember, I was trying to say the milk in my bottle had gone off and they thought I was just being bad.

It's very rare I get any hugs and I don't have any toys. It's okay though, they need the money more than me, to take away the pain. I don't know where the pain's coming from though. Dad put mum into hospital a couple of times. I don't understand to be honest. They're not really cut out for this and I'm not enjoying any of it at the moment. I don't know what I've done wrong. That's all I think about between crying and being shouted at all day. Both of them have problems and because they're my mum and dad I've got an even bigger problem.

Our children

Dominique and Raymond were great together and when they had Jack, well he was just the icing on the cake. Wonderful things kids, aren't they? They are amazing from the moment they're conceived. They are like sponges, they're so quick at picking things up. Jack was doing things long before he should have been. He was bright, smart as a button and he had the biggest smile in the world, he was truly the son they had always wished for. As a small child his favourite programmes were *Postman Pat* and *Fireman Sam*. He was counting and saying words before he knew his ABC. He could identify different colours at an early age too. As he grew older he liked fixing cars with his dad and his favourite football team was Manchester United, just like his dad, who he idolised. He was never a problem, he grew into a charming young man and was now ready to spread his wings in the big wide world.

He had met a quiet gentle girl called Stephanie; she was sweet and she came from a good family. Dominique and Raymond welcomed her into their home, they loved her. With his parents' backing and approval, Jack set up home with her and it wasn't long before they had their own good news. They had a little girl called Sam. Stephanie would visit Jack's parents on a Wednesday, every Wednesday. Then on one particular occasion they noticed her eye was bruised. They asked her what had happened and she said she had been clumsy and had walked into the kitchen

they are not. If we want them to act in a particular way, we have to behave in that way. We must lead by example.

What we don't know

Body imaging

Guptar Singh was crushed in a seven car pile up in the centre of London on January 14th 2007. What's mysterious about this is that his friend Gregory Smith said that was impossible as Guptar was on a plane heading for Mexico with him at the time, which was proven by video footage taken at the airport. Somehow, we are led to believe, the video was accidentally erased by security staff just before the information was to be seen by the world's press. With no trace of the video, Gregory's story could not be collaborated and he was labelled a madman. Gregory also said that the real Guptar Singh was kidnapped, right before his eyes, by several men in black suits and dark shades.

Meanwhile back in London, four independent witnesses testify to seeing someone that looked exactly like Guptar in the crushed vehicle just before dying. But they say, although it looked like him even down to the tattoos on his body, he spoke in a tongue which was unknown to humans, so it could not have been him. They passed the information on to officers from the Metropolitan Police, but no one ever came back to see them about the incident, and the car, along with everything else, was taken away by the army who were on the scene in seconds, even before ambulance crews could arrive or news cameras.

So my question to you is, if that wasn't Guptar Singh who was killed in the car crash then who the hell was it?

Undercover rogue operatives call it *body imaging*. This is where extra-terrestrials take on the form of humans to infiltrate the planet so they can go undetected and eventually rule the earth. This information is classified top secret. If the general population were to get a wind of this, there would be worldwide panic. Until a war is declared, they live in our communities and are in our everyday lives. The imaging is so sophisticated now that they can be amongst us and go virtually unnoticed. The good news is that they are already here and have not yet launched an attack. However the bad news is, when they do, we will be powerless and at their mercy.

It's hard to tell who is who when most of us spend all of our time hiding behind an image.

The other baby

How do you think the other baby is doing?

The one which wasn't to be spoken about, the one you were never supposed to mention or acknowledge. Those were the conditions, if you were to continue to live at the family home. You were never to speak of her or have any contact with her or the woman you betrayed your wife for. You were told you were not to even look at them, if you saw them in the street. Well, you stuck to it and throughout the years you got more and more used to it, but still, every now and then, you must wonder what you missed out on?

What she looks like, how she is, what happened to her, did she do okay for herself? Especially now since you and your wife ended up going your separate ways and now she is pregnant expecting someone else's baby. What price did you pay for your minor indiscretion?

Sorry I meant to say, what price did your baby pay?

The one no one acknowledges or talks about?

Crystal ball

I didn't get a job because Sue the clairvoyant told me I would inherit a million pounds on December 21st. That was nine years ago. Who knows, it could still happen. I liked Elliott, but I didn't give him a chance because she said she could see a dark side in him and anyway I would meet a kind, handsome stranger. I haven't met one yet. I had booked a trip to go to Egypt with my sister, but Sue talked me out of it. She said the timing wasn't right, it would have been a disaster.

I went to see Sue so she could tell me about my future. I was confused and unhappy at the time and I found some of the good things she said comforting, like when she told me my aunties and cousins who had passed away were still nearby and putting bright rays of sunshine around me. That made me feel warm. And when she told me I would pass my driving test and I did, and I would pass all my studies with flying colours and, I can't believe it, I did that too.

Some of the things she mentioned, no one could have known, but there were also things she said to me that didn't happen and when they didn't I felt let down and disappointed. I was frightened of making decisions for myself. But I'm not any more.

Now I don't live my life for tomorrow, I live it for today, because who knows what tomorrow might bring?

Memories

I remember

Things I remember... I remember my first crush. I was about nine years old. She was called Melanie. She had flaming red hair. She used to chase me around the playground. I used to pretend to be angry about it, but I liked her chasing me. Boy was I in love with her!

And I remember family life growing up. We were poor, but there was still a tremendous feeling of togetherness. We made do and we were all right, we were. I remember when the King of rock'n'roll died and when Bob Marley died. I remember going to the school dance when I was in my final year. I was so grateful mum had got me the outfit I so wanted. I knew she had nothing and yet she really went out on a limb for me.

I remember my first love and when I lost my virginity. I also remember when I first had my heart broken. I'll never forget that. I remember my first job and how nervous I was. I remember when I passed my driving test and buying my first car and when my friend Tony died of cancer. That was an awful period. I'd never seen a dead body before.

I remember when I first went on an aeroplane and I went to the Caribbean. The exhilaration and happiness I felt... I thought things couldn't get any better. That is until the arrival of my daughters Jessica and Natalie, those were monumental moments in my life. There are a few other things I remember, but not a whole lot more to be honest. I didn't create many great memories. I didn't do a lot of travelling, so there was still plenty of the world I never got to see.

Mostly I remember a lot of unpleasant things, stuff I don't want to remember. That's when most of the years seemed to blend and mould into nothingness. There certainly wasn't as much laughter as there could have been and I didn't do half of the things I could have done and I let opportunities go, one after another. What a fool I was. I can't get that time back. In many ways, I let things slip right past me.

What are you going to remember in your old age when you look back?

Looking back

The years have flown by, especially the last twenty. They've gone in a blink. I'm in my forties now. If I was to close my eyes, by the time I opened 'em up again I might miss the next twenty and be down the graveyard! It's gone that quick. I always wanted to do something good with my life. I wanted to do something history- defining like Nelson Mandela, locked up for twenty-seven years in prison. Look at the humility he showed after being incarcerated all those years... no bitterness, so humble. Or Muhammad Ali, when he took a stance and wouldn't fight in the Vietnam War, or Bob Geldof, raising money for Africa. The truth is, I feel like such a failure. I couldn't even make it as a singer. Fifteen years I dedicated to the band and we didn't even release one single. The best we ever played at was Deighton Working Men's Club. All those wasted years and the thing about it is we were pretty decent. What do you think it is that they have, those stars? What's the magic they have? It's an enigma. What's the secret? How do you become one of the élite? Why do some people succeed in life and why do some people just remain dreamers like me?

I sit at home with our Angie and I think back to when I was a young lad. I love Angie and she's been good to me, but I didn't handle things well. I put her before the music, so I never did all I could to get where I wanted to be. I never put all of my energy into it. I suppose, if you're not really going to give something a hundred per cent and you're only doing it part-time, you might as well not do it at all really. Still, I've got my memories. I can't stop thinking though if I'd played my cards differently where I might be today. I love our Angie, but I put her before my dream and I can't turn that little voice off in my head which says that was a mistake. I should have gone for it, I had the talent, I know I did. It wasn't Angie's fault, it was mine. Never mind, I've missed that boat now, but if you get a chance and you can do something, make sure you give it your all because that little voice which says you can do it never goes away, and at least you'll know then, whether you do have what it takes. Just give it your best, that's my advice.

Seven days a week

If I didn't laugh, I'd bloody kill myself. The place was like a bomb site two minutes ago, but it's coming up to visiting time now so they've just absolutely blitzed it. I need one of those surgical masks, it absolutely pongs of air freshener. Workers on duty today are Annalise, Lisa, Jeremy, Sarah and Claudine, Rota 1 in short.

We are all sitting in the living area, all made up and paraded for our families to come and see us like dogs from Crufts. Sheila's husband is late again. The halfwit always comes in running, apologising that he's late, briefcase half open, paperwork falling out all over the place, he almost fell into my lap last week. That happens as regular as clockwork. And then there's Wendy's brother Arthur, he's taken all of Wendy's money and her house. He comes in here with his new girlfriend. She has a different outfit on every visit. That's where the money's gone. It's a bleeding outrage. His own sister too.

The staff, instead of being with us, are in the back having their cups of coffee as usual. They think because I have a hearing aid, I can't hear what they say about us. Some of it's not worth repeating. My, oh my, I never thought I'd end up in a place like this, an unwanted commodity sitting on a scrap heap. No one's been to visit me for the last four months and they've all got valid reasons why they haven't. I remember how they sold this place to me. "You'll love it there Mum, you'll meet new friends. You'll have loads to do. You won't be stuck in the house on your own and we'll come and visit you every day. Please, Mum, we'll be more comfortable knowing you're being looked after and you'll have three square meals a day." That's what they said over and over again, that's the pressure I was under. I had to bite my lip. I wanted to say it, but I didn't.

I just wanted to scream at the top of my voice, "Why can't you look after me. I'm your *mum*! Don't put me in a house full of strangers. I can't live with people that don't know me or anything about me. I won't be happy there. It won't be fantastic. I want to be with people I know and around people who are supposed to love me, people whom I have loved and shown nothing but love to." But I didn't and the tears started to fall out of my eyes because I knew my family didn't want me any more and that I was now considered a nuisance. I had become too difficult for them and my husband didn't want me either, so here I am. What can I do about it?

Hold on, it's medication time. "Annalise, can I have some water with my tablets please?" You know sometimes that girl just doesn't think. Sorry, where was I? Oh yes, so here I am. Most of the people, the friends they said I'd have in here, well, their minds have all but gone. They talk absolute dribble and that's just the staff! Ha-ha-ha, no, I'm only playing. No, listen to what I'm saying. All old people need is a visit every now and again, you know. We know you're busy and you're setting the world on fire, but a visit every now and again can work as good as any tablet they give us in here, you know, or warm us up as much as any heating system. It lets us know you're still thinking about us and we haven't been forgotten. It's just something to look forward to so perhaps you'll have a think about it and make the effort. Because we all need someone to talk to, don't we?

Human spirit

Better safe than sorry

Linda was a lovely warm-hearted person. We worked together for a short while back in 1998. The one thing she always talked about was her two children. She would do so with a big smile on her face, they were her pride and joy. Rachel and Marcus. She described them as being her heroes. On a night at work, if things were quiet, we would sit and talk and she would tell me snippets of their lives, so much so that I felt like I knew them personally.

I ended up getting a job somewhere else. I never kept in touch with Linda, but I never forgot her either. I heard from somebody though, some news that disturbed me. I hoped it wasn't true. I heard a group of teenagers were joyriding one night and crashed into her son and daughter who were driving in the opposite direction and they were both killed instantly.

I saw someone who worked at the old building who told me it was true. I was deeply saddened, because I knew how much her children meant to her and I know how that must have ripped her world in two. Unless you get a hurricane in your life, like Linda losing her children, you really don't have anything to complain about.

Some years later on, I was caught speeding, I'm ashamed to say, and I had to go on a road awareness course. The tutor delivering the session that day was Linda. Instead of letting her grief swallow her up, she had become an avid campaigner for safer driving.

You don't have to give up.

Warm souls

Once I met Kristina, I never forgot her. I doubt she would even contemplate that she would become part of my thoughts. She wasn't family, she was just an old lady who lived across the road where we lived, and yet, you see what the power of a smile and a hug can do, it can cause a connection, which stays with you for ever.

I was eleven years old when I met her. She used to invite my brother and me into her home. My mother worked two jobs and my dad wasn't around. Somehow this old lady took a shine to us and would give us sandwiches, biscuits and hot drinks. I don't know why she cared about us, because we weren't her family. I know she's long dead now, because it was years and years ago and she must have been in her mid-eighties even back then and I'm forty-three now. But still, I remember her fondly, that warm smile, those deep-set brown eyes. Her face was aged with the lines of wisdom, but well weathered and alluring in its appearance. She was our adopted angel who made sure no harm came to us.

If I knew where you were, Kristina, I would lay the most beautiful flowers at your grave. If I knew who your relatives were, I would tell them all about you and the things you did for us, but sadly, I do not. So if you are anywhere where you might hear my heart and these words, I just want to say a big thank you for the kindness you showed my brother and me when we were growing up. Thank you. It meant a lot to us and we really appreciated it.

Do not for one minute underestimate what the power of a touch or a kind word and some good feeling towards someone can do for them. I shed tears when I think of how she opened her arms to us. When you receive love and warmth like that, you never forget it.

Years later, in passing conversation, I mentioned Kristina to my mother. She asked me if I remembered her son who was killed in a violent incident when he was cruelly set upon by a gang of thugs in an unprovoked attack. I didn't. I had no recollection at all. Could that have been the reason why Kristina warmed to us? I never recognised her grief, she hid it well. She never spoke of it, but I know that now she will be reunited with her son again and will be happy once more.

RIP Kristina, From my soul to yours – xxx

I knew

I knew I was losing her. It's a horrible feeling to have at the back of your mind, when your partner is pulling away from you and wants to do more and more things without you. It's like a build-up, isn't it? Their tiny feet are beginning to flutter all over again and they want to fly, only this time it's without you. They want you to stay where you are, you are excess baggage; you don't make them smile any more, you do the opposite, you age them. We can only pretend for so long, can't we? (Don't say you haven't noticed there has been a change in their behaviour. You might have to start all over again soon. It's not something to look forward to, is it, entering the dating game once more, and at your age! It's depressing to even think about, isn't it?) I could feel I was losing her, the writing was already on the wall; we were just playing out the scenes telling each other no matter what we'd be together. But when we faced our own side of the bed, that's when our true feelings would come to life and the thoughts would start flying at 100mph. Why are we the way we are with each other? Why does it have to be like this? Unanswered questions, emptiness and doubt, then eventually it happened. I knew she would leave before she even left. This is what I feared, and it happened. Sometimes there's just something in the air that makes you know, and then the game is up.

We can get over pain, and we can find love again.

124

Time sweet time

This is a true story. Now, my partner and I had just split up in 2001. I went to America to get away. I admit I wasn't coping very well. I kept playing the same things over and over again in my head. It can't be, but it was true. We were finished for good this time. I had booked myself a holiday. It was the first time for me going abroad, going on a plane, and I was going on my own.

We had been travelling for about eight hours when the pilot made an announcement saying we were going to experience a lot of heavy turbulence, but there was nothing to worry about. Everyone was looking around at each other for reassurance, but I couldn't have cared less if it went down. I felt like I was dead anyway.

I was very low, but timeout in America helped me a lot; being away from my usual circle, not having to see my ex, getting time for some breathing space. I was out there for three months altogether.

Coming back to the UK I had time to think about my life and cool my head down a bit. On the way home, the plane started shaking like mad again, only this time my words to another passenger were, "Is the plane going to be okay? It is safe isn't it?" I wanted to live again.

I guess the point I'm trying to make is no matter what problems we have, and no matter how severe they are, time heals everything. We just have to allow time to do what it needs to and things will get better, we just have to be patient.

Lessons

Millionaire stories

I got loads of girls on the go. I love it–Oh my gosh, all this totty. Ha-ha. I left Monica's house, then I went to Lisa's house. I love Lisa's cooking. After Lisa's house, I went to Susan's house. I love Susan's body. After Susan's house, I went to Leyla's house. I love how Leyla can talk. She knows so much about so many different things. This is the life.

I tell 'em all, my job involves working away from home. I work in construction, which is the perfect excuse for me not to be around all the time. "That's how I can get away with it," I tell the ladies. I can be working away for a week at a time all over country, then I'm on to the next one. But some way, some how, our Sonia found out about everything. I don't know who told her. I said, "I'm sorry."

She won't return my calls. I don't care about the other girls, but she won't listen to me, she won't talk to me. What have I done? What part of the story is this? This, Romeo, is the part of the story where you lose everything. This is the part the guys always leave out when they're bragging about their conquests, tapping you on the shoulder, having a laugh with you, telling you what a big stud you are and giving you all the high-five stuff.

If I had a penny for every story I'd be a millionaire.

Elisabeth and Robert Mortimer

Elizabeth Mortimer told Robert Mortimer, "I thought when we got married you would put one hundred rose petals in my bath every night. I thought you would sing to me, serenade me, make me feel special. Why did you ask me to marry you, if you were not prepared to be thoughtful and romantic?"

Robert replied and told Elizabeth he did not expect to do a full day's work and come home to no hot meal, and still be expected to be romantic. He also said he thought after they got married that Elizabeth would stop shying away from the kitchen and start cooking like all of his friends' wives did. He looked at her.

Elizabeth told Robert she was disappointed that he thought she should spend all her time in the kitchen and informed him he was quite capable of being able to prepare a meal for himself. She and Robert had a turbulent relationship and on occasions would not talk for days at a time. Elizabeth realised she had been influenced by what she thought a marriage should be and not actually what a marriage was.

If a lot of people discussed what their expectations were before they got married, they'd probably still be married now.

Be realistic.

The future

Alec Reed always laughed at those who were less fortunate than himself. "Look at them, look how stupid they are. Look!" He used to tease people who had disabilities and call them spastics and say they were weird. He did not feel ashamed of his behaviour, mimicking those who were physically or mentally challenged. He would say to his friends, "Look how stupid these people are. Look at that one in the wheelchair. I bet he wishes he had powerful legs for running like me. And look at him with the funny eyes and nose. I bet he wishes he was as handsome as me. And look at that girl, how she walks dragging her foot; she looks like a zombie. Hee-hee-hee."

One night, after he had been out drinking, he decided to cook himself a meal. However he fell asleep whilst doing so, and his pans caught on fire and then his house. He was severely burnt. Up to seventy per cent of his body was covered in third-degree burns. That night changed him for ever. He was furious, because not only did he have to come to terms with his own injuries, but he also had to come to terms with the dreadful way some people behaved towards him. He couldn't understand how they could be so insensitive, how some people were so cruel and would spend all their time staring at him. He hated it. He would scream at them, "Why are you all looking at me?" It made him very upset, but then he remembered how he used to behave before the fire.

Be careful how you treat people, because in the same circumstances you never know how they will treat you.

Then there was none

Wealth at last, money at last, fame at last. When this happened, Hugo got himself a brand new car for £250,000. This was his personal reward to himself for his hard work. Then he got himself the type of house he always wanted, one costing nineteen million. Previously he had been renting a one bedroom flat for £50 a week. How things had changed. He had come up in the world. What he had done was the equivalent of striking oil in the Sahara desert. New things, new life. He had a look at what else he could improve on. He had a look at his partner, Emily. He had been with her since he was a young kid in short trousers. He thought about it and he thought he must keep her, she had been the one consistent thing in his life that had been good for him.

His work took him to places he had never seen before. He was surprised by all the reaction to his new-found stardom. He went from having five friends, to having five hundred friends. He was delighted. It was unbelievable. He now had five hundred genuine friends. The bands were constantly on tour, on the road from one town to the next. He rang Emily at first to tell her he missed her, but then the calls got fewer and fewer. At the concerts, women would scream and swear their undying love to him. At first, he ignored their advances, but when he met Cassandra she was Sexy with a capital S. On meeting her, he told his security people to ask Emily to leave their home and to leave her keys behind. He went from being charming and patient to being rude and obnoxious.

He bought his friends Lamborghinis, Ferraris, aeroplanes and houses. He bought and bought until there was nothing left. And a funny thing happened, because when he had spent all his money, one by one all of his genuine friends disappeared, including his new beauty queen Cassandra. Then, he had nothing.

This is Hugo's story, but it could almost be anybody who achieves success. You don't have to lose your identity or lose who you are because of it.

The party

Kathryn asked Joe to book the party for his sixteen-year-old daughter, but three weeks before the party was due he still hadn't done so. Joe told her to stop worrying, he had everything under control and Kathryn just had to trust him. She was his daughter too and there was no way on earth he would let her down. Kathryn begged and urged him to do it now, but Joe kept putting it off. He said he would do it at the weekend, but when the weekend came, he said he was going to help his brother fix his car. Then he told her to relax and said he had booked a day off work. He assured Kathryn that would be the day when it would be done but he ended up reading a book instead.

There was always something else that got Joe's attention, day after day. Eventually, to stop Kathryn asking him all the time, he told her everything had been taken care of and it was all booked. However, three days before the party Joe had finally woken up and was panicking. He tried to book the hall for his daughter's birthday, but someone else had booked it one hour before him and put a deposit down straight away. So the party for Joe's daughter had to be cancelled. She was upset and everyone else was too, including family and friends that had travelled to be there for her special day. Joe was just too cool and laid back about the whole event and in the end it was his downfall.

Waiting around doesn't make things happen, doing what you're supposed to does.

Perfection

Laura Shaw wanted to meet the perfect man. She went out with Bob Larkins for a while, but when he was thirty minutes late to pick her up from her friend's house, she realised he wasn't perfect. She couldn't be with someone like that, he wasn't perfect. It was over.

Then she went out with Larry, Larry Rhodes. They enjoyed each other's company tremendously and were often in fits of laughter together and he treated her like gold. He was a hardworking man and he liked to spoil and lavish her with expensive gifts, but when the carpentry firm he worked for suffered and went down like many other businesses in the area and he lost his job, she left him. She couldn't stand it. Her whole image of him had been shattered. She found out he wasn't perfect. She was very upset, but she realised it was hopeless to try to continue the relationship. Larry just wasn't who or what she thought he was. He wasn't perfect either.

If you keep looking for absolute perfection, be prepared for disappointment. You'll be on your own for a very long time because none of us are.

Money and power

You prayed that one day you would be a rich man – and it happened, but it changed you for the worse. It made you unkind. You had so much money, but what good did it do? What on earth did you do with it? You never helped anyone. You saw people in need and diverted your eyes. You watched your own daughter suffering, when you could have stepped in and eased her pain, but you chose not to, because you said she was marrying beneath her, because she dared to follow her heart and not your commandments. You refused to speak to her again, and now time has passed. Look around, what do you really have in your final years? Yet you still maintain the same position. You are a hardened man, Henry Harper, old age has not softened your temper. Are you content, was it worth it? I wonder what it is you think about, what drives you. Where are your friends, your family? Any of them, your children, your grandchildren, where are they now? Your house is empty and no one visits you. When you became rich, that's when your problems began. You just couldn't see it, you tried to control and overpower everyone around you and for that you have paid the cost and learned an expensive lesson. Money cannot buy you happiness. We all need money to live, but we do not all live for the love of money.

Alone, money will not make you happy. It's the good you do with it that can. If you do no good, it will not enhance your life.

Trust

How can you say you trust when you clearly do not? How can you say you trust your friend, when you will not have him around your woman? How can you say you trust your brother, when you would not give him the loan he promised to return to you? Are these sentiments simply words we band about loosely to others, when we do not engage in the meaning ourselves?

When we trust and we are hurt, it is because we believed in someone and it was revealed to us that the person is not trustworthy. It can be very damaging and painful to us. We feel foolish as though everyone knows that this person wasn't to be trusted apart from us and that everyone is laughing at us. We can be tormented by these emotions and it can take a long time to come to terms with what has happened, especially if the person asks for forgiveness and ask us to trust them again.

It can be extremely difficult to allow oneself to be vulnerable again, to hang on to every word again, to totally believe again. No, we will never do that, no matter how much we say we will. No, we will never do that, so now things cannot be how they once were and trust has gone. It is lost and, worst of all, it may never be found again. We have to wait and see.

Remember what's important to you, keep the trust. Trust is not something we give away freely, it has to be earned.

Burning bridges

Victoria had always had dreams of becoming famous. She had been singing in the shower since she could remember, She was always one for buying the latest teen magazines. She would dream every day of being the next person to take the pop world by storm. She had entered a singing competition and got through to the second round. She couldn't believe it. She reported the news to everyone she knew and they were all very happy for her. However, within a short period of time she started to question what others around her were doing with their lives. Were they just going to carry on living a mediocre existence or were they going to try to better themselves, like she had tried to do?

She started to think her job was meaningless. She stopped focusing on her duties because she was sure it would only be a matter of time before she would be discovered and become an international superstar and have her name up in bright lights everywhere. She became so ecstatic thinking about it that one day she stopped her boss out of the blue and told her she could stuff the job, that it was beneath her as she was going to be the next biggest thing to hit the UK. She said she was in the final of another, singing competition which would be a springboard for her name to be known all over the world. She let her boss know exactly what she thought of her management skills, too. She told her she was inept at her job and didn't even have the supervisory ability to manage making a round of coffee.

She also wrote her boyfriend a lengthy text message saying the relationship was over. Although he had been good to her and she did love him, she thought he was a non-achiever and she wanted to meet someone who had some drive and ambition to be successful. She also said she wanted to meet somebody who was more attractive to her.

On the day of the competition, Victoria's voice was rusty and out of tune. She felt rough, because she had been drinking and celebrating the night before instead of working on the songs she had to do. She had rehearsed her winner's acceptance speech. Well, the competition was fierce and to her shock she was knocked out in the first round. She was a good singer, but there were just some better ones on the day.

Victoria couldn't believe it. She was totally stunned. She made a call to speak to Mary, her old boss, and asked her how she was doing and, if they were still struggling on the line, could she have her old job back? Mary asked her why she would want to do that if the job was beneath her? Surely she would be too busy anyway on one of her worldwide tours, mixing with the likes of Madonna, Beyoncé and Elton John. Mary told her "absolutely not!" She had been very cruel and rude to her when she had only ever shown her kindness and it was too late now. In any case, though they had struggled for a couple of weeks they had now managed to fill her position so there was no possibility of her returning.

On hearing the bad news, Victoria got in contact with her ex-boyfriend, Jenson, and told him she really missed him, and that she had been foolish. She begged him to take her back. He said he had been devastated when he got the text message, not just by her words but the manner in which she had broken the news to him, the fact that she didn't see anything wrong with sending a text. But, it had woken him up. It had opened his eyes for once and made him see they weren't right together. He said he wouldn't take her back, but he wished her every happiness for the future.

Victoria is still single and unemployed. It's been four years now and she wasn't the music industry's next big thing after all. She now knows you have to become a diva before you behave like one.

Don't burn your bridges before you've even built them!

How do you like it?

How do you feel now? Was it all worth it, for you to shit all over your family? Is it the outcome you wanted? Do you know your kids hate you? Yes, I told them what you did. I know you would have liked a nice rosy story to feed them, to explain why you can't live with Mummy any more, but no, I've been left in this and I didn't ask for any of it. I actually believed you when you said you were working late in the office, "meeting deadlines" you said. You must have both pissed yourselves laughing at me, so why should I clean up your mess? As if I'm not destroyed enough. Why should I protect your image?

Thomas was angry at me. He thought I forced you to leave. All his anger was aimed at me, whilst you were getting to keep your halo, held in the same perfect position as always. I just thought no, why should I be left with all the crap, it wasn't my doing. This is all you, Richard. They couldn't understand, they were just crying all the time. So I told them both the truth. "Daddy didn't think what he had at home was special enough."

Your mistress, that vile woman, your lover, actually came to my workplace and told me how long she had been seeing you. Eighteen months sleeping with her behind my back. She told me you didn't love me, you loved her and that you had actually fallen out of love with me years ago, you'd just been hanging around for the sake of the kids.

It came from her. I had to hear it from her. Why couldn't you have spoken to me? We might have been able to work something out. We might have been able to do something, counselling, I don't know, anything. Why couldn't you talk to me? Your girlfriend just blurted it out in front of everybody. I was so humiliated I didn't know what to do or where to turn. I was so embarrassed, I just broke down.

All the wasted years. Was it that really that bad for you? Did you detest me that much? Was I really that dreadful? Was it that terrible being with me? I want you to know I wish you the best with her. I know you're going to need all the wishes you can get, you bastard. Oh there's no fool like an old fool, Richard. Do you think with all the hair dye in the world that you can actually turn the clock back? Does she know you suffer from arthritis, and chronic back pain, and indigestion, and have to take tablets for flatulence – or are you hiding all your symptoms behind your new sports car?

Well you'll see, mark my words, maybe not just yet, but you'll see, one day your fancy bit of skirt is going to let you down and let you down in the worst way. I've seen her type before and she's going to trade you in for a younger model, just like you did with me, when she realises she doesn't need a grandad and that she wants to be with someone her own age.

I want you to think about me and think about what you put your children through, your own flesh and blood. I want you to remember how you devastated our lives for your own selfish needs. I was looking after our children, *your* children. If you wanted a gymnast in the bedroom, you could have lifted a finger to help me out in the house once in a while. Every time I see you, it makes my skin crawl. I can smell her cheap perfume all over you. It's disgusting. I know you'll be sorry. It's just a matter of time, but when that day comes, please don't ring my phone. I will not be nursing you back to life. You made your choice, just enjoy it while it lasts, Richard. Enjoy it whilst it lasts.

Richard – *Knock Knock* Hello Elisabeth darling.

Elisabeth – What on earth are you doing here?

Richard – Mmm, there's no other way of saying this. I've been a complete fool. She's left me for one of the fellas at the gym. Is there any way we can have a talk, love?

Weigh up what you stand to lose before it's gone for ever.

They say love is pain

They say love is pain. And I love her. More than she could ever know. I love her. But I have wounded her deeply. I cut her heart with my bare hands and without any anaesthetic. I have watched her choke and seen the torment in her, by my foolish actions. Now trust is the biggest factor between us. I have been on bended knees, sworn on everything. It has had no effect. Now the relationship has a cancer-like tumour growing within it. We argue more than we make love. I told her "nothing happened". She can't or won't believe it. "Something must have," she says. And we are right back where we started. I don't know how to reach her any more. She rejects my pleas, rejects my advances. Now, I'm scared that any contact with her and I'll say the wrong thing, hit a nerve, and everything between us will disintegrate. A moment of weakness and stupidity that wasn't even acted upon has put me here, so I tell you to act with caution before you look to someone else outside your relationship to provide comfort to you, before you go down the same path as me. I mean when the news came out about the other woman it was at a time when everything between us was wrong. I had gone out for the day I was unaware my phone had slipped out of my trouser pocket and landed on the chair. It was in plain view, just staring at her, asking her to pick it up. I imagine how enticing it must have been; I guess an opportunity presented itself and was one she could not resist because she read each and every message one from the lady in question; her reading that particular message would end up changing us for ever. I tried to talk to her plead with her as I was guilty of being a fool; I had done wrong – I had engaged in conversation with her, but I was not guilty of having an affair as it had not progressed. I knew the text looked incriminating but it wasn't as bad as it appeared to be; I hadn't met her but nevertheless I couldn't categorically prove I hadn't. Too late, because it's a war every single day now and of course the situation wasn't helped by the details of the other woman having been so viciously delivered to her. A friend of hers added her piece and said how could he do this to you and that's all she needed to hear.

"Liar, liar, I can't trust you. I can't believe anything you say any more. I can't believe anything you say. You are a liar. I can't believe a single word." That was the side effect of my behaviour. It changed us completely. Then came the suspicion, anger, confusion and rage, the monitoring, the analysing, double checking, triple checking; everything I did came under a microscope. There couldn't be a hair amiss. Sometimes there would be peaceful moments but they were still marred by a deep underlying sadness. Then we'd be right back to suspicion, anger, confusion, hurt and rage all over again.

Think twice before you think of hurting a loved one, because it's quite easy to destroy a relationship, but very hard to fix one.

Changes

Kelly: Thanks Mum, thanks Dad, I think I'm ready for going back home now. I feel much stronger. I'm never going back to him. I'm going to live my own life and the way I wanna now.

Dad: Why don't you stay a bit longer, darling? There's no rush, you stay with us as long as you need to, petal.

Kelly: No, Dad. It's time I was going back home. You'll be glad to have your bathroom back on a morning, won't you?

Dad: I suppose so darling, if you're sure.

Dad (later): Don't you think it was a bit odd, love, our Kelly being so quick to want to leave again?

Mum: No, I think she just wants us to have our house back and maybe a bit of space for herself as well. She's okay now, isn't she?

Two weeks later

Dad: Oh no, Terry said he saw the both of them on the boulevard earlier today. She's back with him again, Susan, after everything he's done to her as well. I can't believe it. She must need her bloody head examining, well she may be fooled by him, but if I ever catch him round here again...

Mum: She needs our support, Nigel, she's still our daughter.

Telephone rings

Kelly: Mum, can you talk? Dad's not there with you is he? Can you talk in private, Mum?

Dad: Who is it, Susan? Is that our Kelly? Let me have a word with her. I'll tell her what I think of her set up. I won't mince my words either.

Mum: No, it's not. It's just someone ringing again about a survey on what washing powder I use, Nigel. Calm down.

Dad: Put the phone down. Let 'em bother someone else.

Mum: Stop being horrible, Nigel. I'll take it in the kitchen.

I can speak now, darling. I'll have to whisper though, your dad's here, but I've gone into the kitchen. Wait, I'll just shut the door.

Kelly: He's bought a ring for me, Mum. He said he's been heartbroken this time. He's not been able to sleep. Things are really going to be different this time, they really are.

Four weeks later

Kelly went back to Jacob, but almost as soon as the door was locked he was the same way with her as he had always been. He spat and cursed at her for up and leaving him and going to her parents. He made sure she got the message well and truly and she was back in his clutches. Once again, she wished she had never gone back.

As small children, we are told not to put our hands near the fire and if we do we find out for ourselves... we end up getting burnt. So why as adults do we think things are any different?

Trials

Frank was working hard. He was having to balance his relationship, his job and doing some extra studying for a course he had been sent on, which was going to be good for his personal development, as well helping out with the children on a daily basis. So he was exhausted. He woke up one morning, phoned work and told them he had the flu. He was sick and he needed a rest. He told his wife Diane he needed a break from her too and the everyday chores he had to do.

She said, "Well what about the children? You can't just take a break from them." He said he would be in touch in the near future. That was over three years ago and he has been resting ever since. He never went back to work. He got used to being off and having no responsibilities. He just asked his doctor for a sick note. Time and time again he would claim he was unwell. Of course there was nothing wrong with him. He had all the rest he needed, but it came at a cost. It's as if he travelled in a time capsule back to the 1980s, because he is now living at home with his parents again. The ironic thing about it is he now wishes he had never taken the rest and he had stayed busy.

He had liked his time being occupied. He had liked the course he was studying and his place of work and he had liked waking up to his wife and children every morning. He can't do any of those things now, because one morning he got up and said "I quit." That was the same week in which he was going to be informed he would be getting a promotion. It was also the week his wife was told she would be getting more hours at work, which would have eased their financial worries, and also the week her mother told her she wanted to spend more time with her grandchildren, so she was going to start having them during the day on a weekend so she and Frank could have time together. Diane was excited about letting Frank know this but he walked out on everything just before she had the chance to tell him. So he never knew.

The trials and tribulations we have to face can be very difficult. Look at Frank, he wanted a break, now he has all the time in the world to rest. He says it is the last thing he wants to do. He wants to be busy. So was this simply a test of endurance for him? I think so.

If we are willing to persevere, there can often be a valuable lesson to be learned. If we say the test is too much for us, we cannot become stronger and grow from it and we do not find out the true meaning of why we were given the test in the first place. There is a lesson to be learned in all we experience, good or bad.

Illusions and Trickery

No guarantees

I tried to ring your phone, there was no answer. It's not like it was disconnected, it just said *the number you have rung is no longer in service*. Please tell me what's going on. I went to your home after trying to contact you. I was waiting to hear from you. There was no furniture at your address, no curtains, no nothing. It's like no one ever lived there. I don't know what to do. You said it was just a minor problem: a cheque hadn't cleared at one of your firms overseas, and until it did you were in a bit of a mess. It was nothing to worry about, you said, it was simply an error made by Camille, your secretary, a sixty-five-Year-old lady who you should have dismissed a long time ago, but you saw it as a bad omen because she had been with you from the start.

Twenty thousand pounds is the amount you wanted to borrow. You were embarrassed about it and you made me swear not to tell a soul. It would only take a couple of weeks and I would have all my money back. You asked me to believe in you and I did. You said I was special and although we had only known each other for a short while you wanted to introduce me to your family because you could see me included in your future. So, I went to the bank and took out the £20,000 you needed to pay your staff, but now I can't get hold of you anywhere. Why didn't you say you were moving? Where are you? Where have you disappeared to? You said you loved me and that you would never ever hurt me. That £20,000 was all the money I had in the world. How could you do this to me?

Jean didn't take any precautions, she took all the money she had in the world and gave it to someone she had only known for five minutes. For him it really was too good to be true. No wonder he didn't want her to tell a single soul. There's such a thing as being trusting, but this was something else. If you don't protect yourself, who will?

Human beings say a lot of things. In the end, we do what we want.

Don't leave yourself wide open!

Beware of the wolf

It was me that found her unfortunately. I heard a faint scream and saw her lying in a side-alley. Her skirt was up to her waist... She was moaning. I couldn't believe it. I told her she was safe now: I would protect her. She was a right mess. She had no underwear on. Her handbag with her belongings, lipstick, perfume, were scattered all over the pavement and she was hysterical. I spoke to her and held her hand as I was trying to calm her down. There were one or two people around but all in all the streets were pretty empty, but I did see one guy, a black lad, about twenty-two or three.

He was looking suspicious. He had a hoodie on. I mean, what was he doing out at that time of night? When I shouted "Get him, he did it!" at the top of my voice, he just ran like the clappers. Someone tried to apprehend him, but he was just too fast. But he musta been guilty, right, or why else would he have run? It came out later when he was picked up that he was a filthy stinking drug dealer called Delroy Evans with priors for shop thefts and burglaries. There was no forensic evidence linking him to the crime, but the victim said she'd got a good look and it was definitely a black guy.

I was in the local papers, *Hero comes to rescue of rape victim*. They talked about how I went into the ambulance and hospital with her and supported her. My family were really proud. I had a picture with the local Bobbies as well under the banner of *hero*. They treat me like a superstar round where I live. I always wanted to be famous. In fact when I was young and growing up, I always used to do impressions of celebrities and I was really good at it. In fact, some say with a bit of fortune, I might have even made a career as an impressionist. I could do any accent; that was my thing. I'd practised since I was seven years old. I could do any accent, even a Jamaican accent, and I had told Michelle, that's the name of the lady that got raped, before the ambulance arrived that "it's very hard to prove rape". She told me she didn't really see the face of the guy as he grabbed her from behind but before he attacked her, she heard his voice when he put the knife under her ribs. Apparently he said *luk me na wan kill you but mi will dead you if mi have to so keep ya bumbaclart quiet!* I told her I saw a darkie running away and it must have been him or why else would he run? I gave her his description, the clothes he was wearing that night, his build and his whole demeanour so when he was arrested she picked him out of a witness line up. And then she gave evidence at court against him and he was rightly convicted and sentenced to seven years' custody. Well, you can't go around doing that kind of thing can you? We're living in a civilised society. And me, I still enjoy walking the streets late at night. It gives me a chance to clear my head, get rid of all my worries and look out for any vulnerable women. That's my duty – well I'm a hero aren't I? Haha, just between me and you, I'll let you into a secret, there were only two of us really close to where it actually happened that night and Delroy didn't put a finger on her. I'm still laughing my balls off about it now!

Things aren't always what they seem and they aren't always in black and white.

Do-gooders

She was beautiful, she was innocent, she was a virgin, she was so fresh. I miss the time I spent with her. If I could savour the moment for ever, I would. It's something we both wanted. I had to approach her to start the ball rolling, but we both knew what we wanted. I bought her a teddy bear, a nice fluffy pink one to show her my affection and she must have just melted, because she decided to come with me.

She followed me, back to my car, and we went to a hotel. Once there, I lit a few candles and we had dinner. We had roast duck, vegetables, salmon pâté and a big bottle of the finest house champagne. We stayed in the hotel for the next forty-eight hours. It was incredible, one of the best times of my life. Only, as things started to get very steamy again, the door was kicked in by police. There were loads of them. I had never seen so many police. They were swearing and shouting and being overly aggressive. They really hurt me, putting me into handcuffs. They didn't care about her, she was hysterical. She ran straight to them, she was screaming and crying. I think they really upset her, by the way she was acting. I was bundled into a police car.

When I was at the station, they were calling me all sorts of names and threatening to beat me up, all because her parents had made it into something ugly. Because she hadn't come home as expected, they'd got the police involved. I was forty-five and she thirteen. But they didn't give her enough credit, she was old enough to make an informed decision for herself, I gave her that respect.

I went to prison and I will probably be on a sex offenders' register indefinitely, but they don't get it. Our families don't get it, nobody gets it. It doesn't sit well with them that we are just the way we are. Society can't accept it, so they put a lot of money into different programmes, to try to cure us, but you can't rehabilitate what can't be rehabilitated.

I sat before a panel before I was released. Basically I told them everything they wanted to hear: that I was sorry for what I did and that I was ashamed that I had hurt a child. I even broke down crying. I knew if I didn't show any remorse, I was never going to be released so yeah, I played the game. Then they started giving me day releases, then weekend releases. I'd go round to the coffee shops, by the local schools, so I could see in the playgrounds. At first that was enough for me, then I wanted more. Before long, I was back to the hotels again with a new girl. I managed to convince them I was a changed man and I was released in 2010. I've got to thank the British Justice System, the Social Workers, the Probation Officers, the Well-Wishers and the Do-Gooders. I've got to thank them for giving me my first chance, second chance and third chance to be staring through your child's bedroom window right now. I'm free...

Growing up

Ego

Back in my day, I used to be a bit of a lad round town with the ladies, but when I met Debbie, all those years ago, I left that lifestyle behind. I wanted something real, something that meant something to me. I was sick of feeling unfulfilled the emptiness the one night stands and to be honest I never looked back, but me and Debbie, we've lost the spark we once had and I've not been happy at home for a while now. So when I saw Kim, I was taken aback. She's smart, she's intelligent, she's sensitive, I can talk to her and she's really down to earth, she's beautiful inside and out and what a smile she has. Furthermore, her figure reminds me of how my Debbie used to look, before she gained the extra pounds.

Everyone likes Kim, all the guys on the shop floor fancy her, and she actually told me I make her day when she sees me on a morning. When she said that to me I was lost for words, I don't know how she is still single. I enjoy seeing her and I think about her before I even get to work. I think I could settle with her, I really do. She's asked me for my number. I told her I was with someone, but that we were going through a difficult patch. I didn't give her my number, but I came close to it.

Debbie and I just argue all the time. Nowadays we hardly even touch each other. It feels like we are dead in the water, but this girl, Kim, she really likes me and I like her.

I just don't know what to do about Debbie, that's what the problem is. I'm confused, she's unhappy, I'm unhappy. I still love her, but we argue over nothing. Maybe we're just not suited any more and I've been thinking that more and more since Kim came onto the scene. Kim could be a second chance for me to get things right and find true love again, but what do I really know about her?

We've had a bit of a flirt together, but that's it, nothing else, and what about Debbie? I still love her, that's never changed. Maybe I don't really want to leave her, maybe it's because I've been getting all this attention from Kim, which is why I feel more confident. If she hadn't been flirting with me, calling me a hunk, would I still feel as strongly about leaving Debbie? I doubt it.

I'm fifteen years deep with Debbie and even if I was with Kim, could I guarantee I would be any happier with her once I got to know her after the honeymoon period was over? I'd be giving up a lot. What if it was to go wrong? Where would I be then? I know myself that I'm not the easiest person to live with and one thing I do know is that Debbie does love me and when I look at things seriously she's not the only one who has gained some extra pounds. I'm definitely carrying more timber than I used to. Who knows, maybe Debbie and I can turn things around. I reckon we could even enrol in a gym together, you know develop a shared interest. I bet we'd have a right laugh as well.

Can I really afford to go with this new girl and gamble everything I have? My home life, the house we have? I like her, but the next time she asks me what I'm doing after work I am going to tell her I'm going out for a romantic meal with my wife and we are going to have a night at a beautiful hotel and a hot soaking bath afterwards and I'm going to suggest to Debbie we go out more often.

I've brushed up my ideas and I reckon I could be more attentive to Debbie and make more time for us to get back to where we used to be. Yes, I think I've come to my senses. I'm not twenty-one any more and I can't afford to lose everything because of my ego. Can you?

A bigger person

Sometimes I watch myself from afar and I see when I am being small-minded and petty or when I am being disrespectful about someone just for the sake of being involved in conversation and being a member of the in-crowd. And I think, *what are you doing?* I might be on the way to work in the morning and spend the whole time trading insults with a colleague about other staff we work with who irritate us. We do the same thing almost five days a week. I don't know what we get out if it; we are just as bad as the people we spend our time critiquing.

Spencer phones me or I'll phone him and we spend our time picking out what we recognise as faults in their make-up. It's often things that I am not that upset about in the first place. I don't like confrontation, so I wouldn't dream of saying half of these things to anyone's face. I'm much more comfortable speaking about them behind their backs. I wouldn't want to offend them. Sometimes when I hear myself going on and my meaningless quarrels, I think to myself, *Can't you be bigger than that? Can't you evolve any more? Do you have to be so petty? Is this you at your highest level? Why not be the person you want to be? Why not be more tolerant, more understanding? Why not try to be that person instead?* That's who I want to be. I have all the wisdom in the world. I can talk with the greatest of them. I just can't put it into practice which in the end is like having no wisdom at all.

Be all you can be, elevate!

Me

I've been able to turn my hand to most things I've put my mind to. I can pretty much do anything. Naomi Campbell and Kate Moss are okay, I must admit, but if I had pursued my modelling career I think they would have been up against it and had some serious competition on their hands. But I decided that going into telesales was more exciting for me, and I'm good at it.

In my work place I've got the best outcomes. We get paid on commission – guess who was top dog in 2008 and 2009? Who else but yours truly. I would have been number one in 2013, 14 and 15 as well, if I hadn't started that stupid college course. Jackie Turner won those years. She's crap at the basic stuff. I feel like without me in the picture to prop her up, she would be really struggling. I'm much better than her, I'm just a lot more professional.

Listen to this, right? I was watching Jamie Oliver's cook-up the other day and I thought what he was doing was soooo easy that I could have done better myself. I could have definitely become a chef if I'd have wanted to. I always got told by my son what a great cook I was but I didn't fancy it; all the shifts they have to work, I couldn't handle it. I like to have a life at the weekend and what a great night I had this one just gone too.

I went to a thirtieth birthday party. I was told my dress looked nice, but it was stunning. It was the best one on the night. My friend Sylvia's dress was okay, she just doesn't have an hourglass figure like me, but who does have anything like me?

Give others a chance to love you as much as you do.

Heaviness

July 1945

Alexander had a secret he couldn't live with because of this thing, this terrible deed he had done, once upon a time. He was no longer his former self, he even looked different because of it. I am not at liberty to say what the deed was. It is not my place to, but what I can say is he tortured himself constantly about it. He was in a never-ending nightmare, a world full of shadows and blackness. He was haunted by it. Part of his brain had shut down because of it, because of what had happened on Sunday 1st July 1945. His speech was affected. He couldn't sleep. He was in permanent torment. The agony was carved deep within his soul for all to see. It was driving him insane. He had tried alcohol and drugs, he had seen doctors, psychiatrists, but nothing had worked. The problem was still there.

He said, "What can I do? I have tried everything. Mother, don't you think I have tried? Do you think I want to be like this?" He shouted as loud as his voice would allow as if to rid himself of the curse of his own conscience. The one question that intrigued everyone was what had he done? I cannot speak of the matter except to say there were hearsay rumours he had treated an old girlfriend shabbily and he had become unwell as a result of it. When she popped into his mind it was a constant reminder for him that would go round and round in his head, over and over again. The lady had found happiness again, she told him this. She had forgiven him, for all the wrongs he had done to her, but he could not break down the walls he had built up in his own mind.

"There is nothing I can do. I am no longer the person I was. I cannot forgive myself." Any potential chance of happiness that came his way disappeared. Even if he did mention his troubles, he was unwilling to let it be part of his past. He hung onto 1st July 1945.with every part of his being. No one could get through to him to say, "We cannot change the past but we can change the future." Instead, he chose to opt out of life and he remained in a world of self-persecution and guilt over something he had done a very long time ago. His demons had him by his throat. All we can do about the past is learn from it, in the hope we will not do the same evils again.

Alexander could not understand this. In the end, it drove him to madness – the booze, the drugs and everything else was just him on a mission of annihilation and self-destruction. It didn't get to the real problem. He said he had tried everything, yes, everything, apart from the one thing he didn't try which was to forgive himself. His affliction consumed every part of his life and, most regrettably, he ended up being detained in a secure unit for the mentally insane and even in his final hour on his deathbed his very last words were *1st July 1945, 1st July 1945, 1st July 1945*, and then he was dead.

Allow yourself to live again. Learn from your past– don't be haunted by it.

The interview

I had just met Jane. She was absolutely wonderful, but it felt like the timing was all wrong. I didn't have anything I could offer her. I was flat broke, I didn't have a penny. I wanted work, I just couldn't find any. I hoped something would change soon. I couldn't even afford to buy her a glass of lemonade when we were out. She was paying for everything and her family were starting to notice. I felt terrible. I needed to find work. I saw a job I wanted and went to see my mate Charles about it. He's an employment advisor. I told him the position I had seen was for a care assistant working at Hollyfield Special Care Unit. He gave me some useful tips for the interview, like maintaining good eye contact, speaking clearly at all times and using my hands to express myself. He said this would show I was passionate about what I was saying. He also told me, what sounded good and what didn't when we practised some roleplay.

The night before the interview, I ironed all my clothes and went over what I was going to say a million times to make sure nothing could go wrong. I went to bed early to get a good night's rest, but I just couldn't switch off and spent most of the night staring at the ceiling. I didn't hear the alarm clock go off in the morning, so when I got up, I was late. Then I was running around like someone possessed. I caught a bus into town and ran as fast as I could. I got there just in time for the interview. I had to wait in the reception area, then I was called up, I was a bundle of nerves. It didn't go too well. I sat in front of four people firing questions at me, and one of the questions I completely misunderstood. I knew by the expression on their faces that I didn't do well.

I went to see Charles. He was excited, sure that I had "done it". Then they rang and told me I hadn't got it. I was crushed. Charles told me to keep my head up and try again. He said, with the kind of enthusiasm I had shown, something was bound to happen for me. A week later another job came up. I went to see Charles again and he gave me some more tips and we went through a mock interview together. I went for the job. I felt a lot more confident this time and I was checking my phone afterwards, going crazy to see if the ringer and the volume were still on. There was no reason why they shouldn't have been. Call it being anxious.

Then they rang. They told me I was successful. I started smiling and I was so happy. But then, the caller interrupted my excitement and said I had been *unsuccessful not successful'*. I had misheard. What a time to suddenly go deaf.

I put the phone down. I rang Charles. He gave me the same advice again; to keep my head up. This time I felt rock bottom. I felt really low, no matter how much I tried it seemed I couldn't get a job. But, I didn't have time to feel sorry for myself for too long, because I was shortlisted for another post. This was going to be the third job I had applied for in as many weeks. This time, I was determined nothing was going to stop me.

I took some of the feedback from the previous interviews and used the information in a positive way. I was really focused and I was adamant I was going to give it my all. This time I answered every question from the interviewers; when I didn't understand one I asked them to repeat it. Initially they had offered me a glass of water which I refused, but when I found one of the questions difficult I asked if I could have that glass of water after all. This gave me some extra time to think and come up with an answer.

It was all over in an hour or so. Later, they rang me to tell me I had been successful. My hearing hadn't gone funny this time, I had done it. I rang my friend Charles to tell him. He was ecstatic! He had believed in me all along. I could hear everyone in the background in his office cheering, because they knew I had been trying my hardest. It paid off for me. If you really want work, you might have to make a job out of finding a job, but it will be worth it in the end.

I can now treat Jane how I always wanted to. We are doing better than ever. We are going away to Rome and we have just put a deposit down for our own house. If I can do it, I believe anyone can. I just had to change my attitude. I'd got used to living on benefits and just surviving, but once I started moving forward there was no turning back.

If you put the effort in today you will taste the rewards tomorrow.

Searching

I love being single. I'm my own boss. I don't have to ask anyone's permission to do what I want, I answer to myself and that's it, nobody pulls my chain, nobody. There's not a single thing I miss about being in a relationship. It sounds empowering doesn't it? If only it was true. I've convinced so many people, I nearly convinced myself. I'm fed up with it all, I go to work, come home and I'm on my own, again and again. And that's my life.

I dream of finding my Juliet, finding love and getting married, but nothing's happened in that department. It's been that way for a long time. Never mind, there are some advantages of having a single life. I just don't know what they are. But I know all about the disadvantages, not having someone to share life's experiences with, not having someone to speak to, be close to, not having someone who understands you and not having someone who loves you. The things some just take for granted.

All my friends are settled and happy and have their own lives. They haven't stood still, they've moved on. Why can't I get a slice of what they have? What's wrong with me? I would love to be in their position. I feel like the loneliest person on earth. I put on a good front and appear as though I'm happy, but that's not how I really feel. I've been patient, I've been waiting and I'm still waiting for something to happen. When am I going to meet someone?

The answer to that is when you meet someone! But if you focus on other things, it won't feel as though you're waiting an eternity.

When

When the sky is black and the clouds hang over your head and no matter where you go they are sure to follow you. When you want to be anywhere but where you are right now. When the postman delivers the news that the job you went for has been unsuccessful and your future is still in doubt. When a day can last for ever and look like the one that came before it. When just getting out of bed can be tiresome. When you're invisible. When no one holds you, no one kisses you, no one touches you, and no one sees you and you go through life unnoticed. When you're falling apart inside and you put on a brave face on the outside. When you wish you could die by natural causes. When there's no rest, no peace and you still can't sleep. When you can't even fake a smile because you have no energy to do so. When the rain won't stop beating down on your head. When there's no solution to your problems. When it's all getting too much and you feel like pulling the plug. When are you going to tell someone how low you're feeling?

This is the time you need to talk to someone.

Across the Pond

Don't judge

Eleanor had always sold her body. Hundreds of men had sex with her over time and she had a reputation throughout the town for being a cheap whore. She was laughed at and made the butt of jokes from the upper-class ladies in the district, who thought she was beneath them, even though most of their husbands visited her.

Though she was a prostitute, and looked down upon because of it, Eleanor had a heart of gold and gave most of the money she made from working the streets on a night towards her grandmother's medical bills. She was a frail old lady in declining health and Eleanor loved her dearly. She was the only person who had been kind to her and showed her genuine love.

Eleanor was a prostitute but she was a million times better than the upper-class ladies and some of the pigs and wild animals she let use her for sex. Her heart was pure and sincere and what many people didn't know was that prostitution hadn't been her choice. Her father was a cruel, vengeful old drunk who pimped her out when she was only thirteen years old, so he could get money for liquor and gambling. So what she did for money was all she ever knew. But alas people did not feel too sorry for her. However, she was determined not to be defined for ever by her past but used the courage and determination it had given her to do what she does now.

Today, Eleanor is the leading professor of science at the Rainbow Academy in Michigan, Tennessee, and her students have the best pass rate in the whole State. They speak of her very highly, about her patience and the passion she has for her work. They say she is able to connect with the students better than any other tutor, because she is able to look deep under the surface and bring out their best qualities. There is even a plaque up in the town she grew up in to celebrate her success – that same town that once dismissed and rejected her.

So before you judge someone, or think you know them, try to get to the heart of the real them because you may find out you don't actually know them at all.

We all have mystery to us; if you look close enough you'll see the real person.

Self-sufficient

John, most winters, had done well from the ranch in providing food for his wife and his two children, John Jnr and Katy Lee. But this winter, they had been unlucky. There had hardly been any rain and the crops had suffered as a result, so John had to ask his friend Jim Shaw, who lived two hundred miles away, for food.

John's brother Brett said he would call at Jim's ranch and pick up the food for them. That was a huge responsibility and John's wife Lillian expressed concerns about placing so much faith in Brett who had let them down several times in the past. He was well known for being a drinker and a notorious ladies' man who had a filly in every town.

On day one, John and his family were anxiously waiting for Brett to arrive with the food from Jim's ranch: some potatoes, chicken, eggs, pig meat and milk. But he never came.

On day two, they were hungry and faint. On day three, the children were hysterical and crying, but there was still no sign of Brett. But, on day four, John had an idea and said to his wife, "I have a healthy horse in the stable, why don't I ride to Jim's to get the food myself?" His wife applauded his suggestion and that's what John did. He went and got the food himself. When he returned home he was weary and weak, but the family ate well and they managed to survive another winter.

If there's something that needs to be done, you may have to do it yourself, otherwise it may never happen. How important is it to have the positive outcome you want? 'John was prepared to starve both himself and his family before it dawned on him to go to the ranch and get the food that they needed. The truth is, his brother Brett was never going to show up. He had got drunk when he was passing through Oklahoma and met up with one of his old lady friends and had completely forgotten his promise to collect the food for his brother and family who were so desperately relying on him and would have perished without it.

The Colour of Skin

Albert Warner hated Negroes. He told his daughter they were uncivilised savages, who ate monkeys' feet and practised black magic. One of his friends from the Klan had educated him on the subject. When his sister Gwendolyn took sick with a severe case of the flu, he sent his daughter Amy to go and look after her. Whilst there, she met Leona, a girl of mixed heritage. They enjoyed each other's company. Amy told her she wasn't at all like her father's description and proceeded to tell her what he had said about Negroes. Leona laughed until she cried at all the rubbish and said it was nothing but mumbo jumbo. Amy laughed too and they became the best of friends.

Amy was introduced to Leona's cousin Winston at one of the clubs. They liked to go to a club called the Marino. She took Amy there to show her that black people were just the same as everyone else and she shouldn't be afraid of them as there were good and bad people in all races. Amy had a fabulous night at the Marino and she danced until her feet were sore. She realised that her father's information had been misguided and incorrect and that Negroes were not out to do harm.

Amy continued to look after her aunty and would ring her father to see how he was doing, but she kept things she dare not mention away from him. She continued to go to club Marino and she and Winston became lovers. That kind of thing was very dangerous then. They had to keep their relationship secret for fear of public outcry.

Amy's father got further into the white supremacy movement. In the end he was totally brainwashed. They convinced him to help them blow up some of the clubs that the Negroes hung out in, one of them being the Marino. The bomb was skilfully planted and when it went off it killed twenty-seven people. Amongst the dead were Winston and Amy. She had just discovered she was pregnant and having Winston's baby. Albert and the Klan members were arrested and sentenced to be executed for the bombing and murders of so many innocent lives. He hated himself for what he had done. He was in deep shock. He did not know Amy went to the Marino. He didn't know about Winston or that she was pregnant. He had killed his own daughter and soon to be grandchild. He loved Amy so much. He questioned why he had ever got involved with the Klan in the first place. He remembered they had approached him when he was vulnerable, when he lost his wife to cancer. That was the year when the Klan came to him and brought out all the hate in him and told him the Negroes were evil and would take everything he owned. He had believed it. They had preyed on his ignorance and exploited it.

Ironically, the Chaplain at the prison was a black man called Everick Jones. He was the first black man Albert had met. The Chaplain asked him to pray with him and repent all his sins before he met his maker. Albert was shaking with fear as the time grew near to his execution. He said to the Chaplain, "How can you forgive me, Everick, when I so callously killed my own daughter and so many of your own people?" The Chaplain said, "What you did was wrong, but you have asked the Lord for forgiveness and welcomed him into your heart. The people that died that day were not my people, they were God's people, just like you and I, Albert Warner. We are all God's people, brothers and sisters."

Albert realised what the Chaplain was trying to say to him and saw it as the truth. For a man's skin colour didn't make him any better or worse than anyone else. It did not show you who he was as a person, it was just the colour of his skin. Albert was then ready to go. He thanked the Chaplain for his blessings and his words of wisdom, for he had been enlightened and was ignorant no more.

Believe in you

Be you

Do I encourage you to do anything at all which doesn't involve me? Or do I become all possessive if you say you want to go out without me by your side? Do I look sad and disappointed? Or do I tell you to go anyway? When you want to have a girly night out with your friends, do I miraculously say I had something planned for us on the same night, or do I let you go? When you say you want to go to your sister's for the evening, is my immediate response to ask what time you will be back? Or is there no time limit? When you say you would like to do something for yourself, do I become distant? Does my whole mood darken or do I say "Enjoy yourself"? When you say you need some time out, do I get annoyed and ask you why you need time out? Or am I gentle and understanding?

If you're living your life for somebody else, who's going to live your life for you?

Waiting game

I couldn't leave then, because it was Craig's birthday. Then I couldn't leave because her parents were coming down from New Zealand. So I stayed. Then it was Christmas. How could I leave then? It would have destroyed the kids. Leo asked me if it meant that his mum and I were going to be a proper family again, and I told him it did. I feel so hemmed in. I'm so unhappy but how can I leave now?

She said we should go and visit her friends more often. I couldn't tell her I just wanted to sit at home and relax for once. I couldn't say I didn't want to visit them. She told me to go for the job she had seen advertised in the paper. I couldn't say I didn't want to change my career. I was happy where I was. I couldn't tell her I didn't want another child either – she was so excited. She told everyone. We were looking for suitable names. I wish she had told me about it first. What could I say to her? The timing wasn't right and it never will be.

In fact it's just dawned on me if I continue to live my life like this, I won't be living it at all. I'll never end up doing anything I want to do. I guess sometimes you have to do and say things even if the timing isn't perfect. I've been waiting for it to be so for ever and the reason I've always missed it is because there's no such thing as the ideal moment. If I don't say something now, I'm starting to think I never will. I don't think I can go on like this; I'm not in control of my own life. I don't feel happy at all and I've now been told something that I believe to be true – that I'm the only person who can change things. If I want to change things that is, I'm still not sure if I want to but I know I should. I'm not going to wait another minute. I'm going to stand up for myself and say something now.

If you don't say anything, how can anything ever change?

Doubt

Doubt stops you from applying that idea you had. It tells you it's unachievable and tells you you're being unrealistic, and you need to come back down to earth. Doubt keeps you strapped in the same position, it makes you question yourself so much that you leave the idea altogether. It steals your energy and takes away your confidence. You can be feeling positive and determined then out of nowhere doubt can jump on your back and wrestle you to the ground, beat you into submission so forcefully that you forget the thoughts you had for ever.

Feelings of doubt are contagious. Other doubters tell those who are unsure that they are doubtful they will ever achieve their dreams and that their plans are unlikely to come to fruition. Some of the best ideas have yet to see the light of day because those who had them were infected by doubt. They told themselves they were just being silly and it would never happen, and those around them echoed their thoughts, so they stopped dreaming and stopped using their imaginations for fear of ridicule. They no longer had aspirations to become what was in their hearts. Well I have some news for you, Thomas Edison invented the light bulb, Alexander Graham Bell invented the telephone and Otis Boykin created a control unit for the heart pacemaker. If any of these men had let doubt take a hold of them then these inventions might never have been created.

If you ignore the doubters, you'll get a lot further in life!

Dreams

Better get what you can in this world, don't pause, don't sleep, don't fall into a coma. Get on with it, because if you don't, *I could have done, I would have done if I had done, I might have done* is the song you'll sing. And you don't wanna have that going off in your head. Try to fulfil your potential, be the best you can be. You're only on this planet for a short period of time, so what you do is important – focus. You wanna be a doctor, you wanna be a lawyer, a teacher, an architect, an astronaut... it's all possible, it's all possible.

What is it you want to do? You can to it. I believe in you. Don't let them tell you that you can't do it. I see what's in your heart, they can't see that. Don't let your neighbourhood define you or your background. Don't use these things as excuses. Even if your circumstances have been rough, don't you still need to move forward? Don't be held back by negative thoughts, they only multiply. You are unique, don't let them tell you a lie, sell you a lie, say you have no right to dream, that dreams are just for them like they have the monopoly on this, don't believe it. You are smart, you are intelligent, you have the ability to do anything. You can fly, if you want to, you just have to plug into the idea, have faith in yourself. Anything worth having is going to take a level of commitment, so take a deep breath and hold on.

Don't let other things overtake what you want to achieve. Don't be side tracked. Concentrate, put the work in now and you'll start scaling the heights of the mountain in front of you, and gradually steps will become leaps and you will begin to move effortlessly closer and closer to your dream. And when you get there, to the thing you want, and you're smiling in disbelief and your heart's beating so fast with the adrenalin rush, I'll be right there beside you. You won't see me or hear me, but I'm going to say it to you anyway. I told you you could do it.

I'm your dream and I can turn into your reality if you let me.

Under a disguise

Freak accidents

Angela Turner died, when the brakes on her bike failed and she went over a mountain cliff. She had been abusing old people in the nursing home where she'd worked for years. She had only had her brakes tested twelve hours before she went on her treacherous cross-country journey. They were working perfectly fine, so what happened? Your guess is as good as anybody's. Then there is Sarah Richardson, who stole money from her disabled aunty's account for over ten years until the chandeliers in her house fell from the ceiling and crushed her. And let's not forget Karl Rivers, who died when a single slate fell off a roof and lodged in his brain.

These deaths sound like freak accidents don't they? Or is there something else going on here? Let me tell you about Karl. He raped a girl thirty years ago and killed her. Her body was never found. He was tried in a court of law, but acquitted, so he walked away a free man. But, unknown to him, he would still have to serve his day in another court, the highest court. Don't think he simply died an unusual death, without reason. That isn't the case. There is something going on here which is bigger than you or me. It's called karma.

We all have to face up to what we have done sooner or later.

Lies lies

What is a lie? A slight distortion of the truth? Something that isn't real? Not a hundred per cent accurate. Some lies are acceptable. For example, a fiancée smiling, white teeth shining, asking what you think of her new dress as she's spinning around and you actually think it is hideous but you say you think it's all right. That's only half lying, right? Because you haven't told her it looks great on her, you limited your enthusiasm, you said it was simply okay. That's an acceptable half lie, committed to protect her feelings. I mean, she seemed so happy, so why spoil the mood. That's not the kind of lie you have lurking in your closet though, is it? No, yours is like a tornado. What is it exactly that you've lied about? What are you so scared of? Go on, you can tell me. What is it in, or about, your past that you don't want anyone to know? Seeing as though we're so hung up on all this honesty stuff, why can't you tell me? Will you tell me? I didn't think so. It's a personal matter, isn't it? We all have skeletons in our closets. Lies are lies and we all tell them. It's just some tell them to a greater degree than others.

Sometimes we have to lie – it would be rude not to.

More lies

A lie is horrible. A lie is not the truth. A lie can come between you and your loved one. If they lie to you, it can break your heart. A lie isn't nice, it's a bastard. If you catch someone in a lie, it will make you question everything they say and do. A lie will look right in your face and smile at you whilst it tries to get past you. A lie is sneaky and thinks it can get the better of you. It thinks it is smarter than you. It doesn't respect you. One lie, two lies, three lies, all of a sudden, they multiply. You have to have a good memory though if you're lying cos you're going to have to remember all your bullshit and remember it line for line.

They say you can spot when someone is lying. You can tell by their body language. It's all nonsense. An experienced liar can look you straight between the eyes and tell you red is green without even blinking, although there will be a time when even the most accomplished liars have their day. That's when the stories no longer add up and all the pieces start falling into place, one after another, until all their lies are exposed.

Did you think you could get away with it for ever? Is it the affair you denied? Does your partner not know the real facts? Is it the robbery you did that you let someone else take the blame for? Whatever it is, your world is going to come crashing down right before your eyes and when it does you'll suddenly get an urge to want to tell the truth and you probably will be telling the truth and you'll be angry and upset that no one will believe you and no one will listen, no matter how loudly you shout and protest. But why should they? After all, you're known for telling lies.

When lies and the truth become blurred, who can you really blame?

What I can't tell you is

Elaine: What I can't tell you is, ever since I found that girl's number in your phone, it has haunted me. I know I told you I was okay and we both agreed we were going to work it out. We have two beautiful young children together who deserve to grow up with both parents. We said we'd get over this and I do, really do, love you, but what I can't tell you is that I still don't trust you. When you were upstairs having a bath yesterday, the one which I ran for you, I was downstairs going through your wallet, looking for any dubious receipts. I don't know what I was looking for; hotel receipts, anything for flowers, jewellery. I really don't know what I was trying to find but something to prove that my instincts are right about you and that you haven't really changed at all.

Sebastian: It's okay darling, because what I can't tell you is that my trust for you was already low since I caught you out in some lies. But since I fucked up with that girl, I trust you even less now. Hey, how does that work? I fucked up. And now I'm paranoid about you. See, on Tuesday, when you said you were going out with your sister Paula for a meal, I thought, that's strange, Paula usually works nights on a Tuesday, so what I can never tell you is that I followed you to the restaurant you were supposed to be at. I got our Jackie to come down and watch the kids for an hour and that's when I followed you. My heart was beating like it was going out of control, because I was sure you were up to something. I had to crawl behind some parked cars on my knees so I wouldn't be seen from the restaurant window, but you were with Paula, just like you said, having a meal. So I rushed back home, thanked our Jackie and three hours later you came home. I kissed you on the cheek, gave you a big hug and said, "Did you have a good night love?"

Elaine: What are we both like? It doesn't matter, because what I can't tell you and will never be able to tell you is that your last couple of bank letters that have gone missing didn't go missing at all. I have them in my handbag at work, I just thought I'd find out the truth, if you were up to something. So I hid them. But when I opened them up later, there was nothing suspicious at all. But I had to know. Something else I can't tell you is I found your new password to your Facebook account scribbled down on a small piece of paper and when you're at your kickboxing class, I read all your messages and see if you have any new friends. I'm looking for girls in particular...

Okay, enough already, you two could go on like this for ever.

If you're not prepared to even trust a little, where can you really go?

Read between the lines

I'm fine, don't worry about me. I'm good, me.

Translation – I am so fragile right now, I could pass out right here.

No matter what happens, I'll always come out the other side, you know me.

Translation – Why can't I get anything right.

I love being single. I'm my own boss. I get up when I want to, I go to bed when I want and I can walk around naked in my own place, if I like. It's up to me.

Translation – I'm sick of being on my own, it's so boring. Why did she leave me? I'm lonely.

Why can't we say how we feel and feel what we say?

Conscience

She was defenceless and weak, she was easy prey for him. He did not care. He did what he wanted, but it was an act which was to stay with him for ever. It would chip away at him bit by bit and still does almost thirty years later to the day.

One night, his own mother fell victim to a violent mugging and was paralysed. He knew what happened. It had just taken so many years to catch up with him. Everyone passed on their sympathies about his mother, but he felt responsible for what had happened to her, like he had done it, with his own hands. Was it linked to his own past? He had never been caught for what he had done all those years ago but now he was having to endure the same pain he had dished out to somebody else's family.

Some things we do we can never take back, they stay with us for ever and remind us that we have a darker side that is hidden. At times, we even try to hide it from ourselves, put it to the back of our minds. No matter where we put it, it's still there and that's the cross we have to bear.

Avoid torment. Mind what you do, because your conscience might never forgive you.

And another thing

Air strikes

They're coming for me. I'm under threat again, I don't even know what this war is about. If I just stay quiet, maybe they won't know I'm in here, maybe they'll leave me alone. This is the tenth time this year I've been under siege. I've been cut, I've had my water pipes cut, bricks and petrol bombs thrown through my window. I can't sleep on a night and because I haven't been able to for the last three weeks now, because of their sustained attacks, I've started to hear voices.

The last time they got to me, they broke my arm. I was in hospital for three weeks and I suffered a mild stroke. That was fifteen months ago. The police went to talk to them down at the rec, where they were all drinking. I could hear one of the officers having a laugh with them. They came back and said they need to catch them in the act as it's just my word against theirs. They need evidence. I think I might have to actually die for anything to happen. You might think I'm in a war zone behind enemy lines or something, but I'm not. I'm at home.

I'm seventy-two years old and I'm having to fight all the yobs on my street. If you can offer me any support, I'd really appreciate it. This is not what I expected later on in life. None of the hooligans work, they just spend their time terrorising me. As for their parents, well I don't see any of them. Until something is done about this, the air strikes will continue. I just want someone, anyone, to come to my rescue and get me out of here. Please, anyone, help, they are going to kill me. Help me.

I wanna tell you a story

What can we really believe? One of the most controversial books ever written is the Bible. Different religions question the authenticity of some of the scriptures in different books and some people have actually been killed when they have dared to question the information that lies inside and it was written thousands of years ago.

I know first-hand a story can change within five minutes, never mind thousands of years ago. What about when someone describes an event, for example, where you were actually present, let's say a disagreement with another friend which you observed where words were traded and they came off worse than the other party but you're surprised on a later date to hear them retelling the story to someone else giving a blow by blow detailed account of what happened only in their new improved version they now paint themselves as the hero been all assertive and powerful and the person they were arguing with as the one who was upset and in tears. It's still a story. And what is a story anyway, except for someone else's version of the truth or what they know it to be? If you weren't there, you have to believe in what you are being told or not believe.

If I told you a story about a garden and I said the grass was beautiful and purple in colour, it may trigger an alarm off upstairs to make you question what I was saying because you know the colour of grass is green, but things aren't always that easy to spot, so all I'm saying is, if someone gives you information, do not merely take it for the truth, but question the fabric of what you are being told.

Unless you were there, well you weren't there...

Bitching

Margaret had planned for everyone to come round to her home for some nibbles and a few drinks. She could see that morale at work was low and there had been some unpleasant times of late so she thought she would do something nice. Everyone was invited. There was Claire, Susan, Terry, Michael, Karen and Angela, Paula, Kylie and myself. It was a good idea, but I was a little bit upset that Angela decided to show up. I mean, why bother! She always had a face like a slapped arse and was as miserable as sin. I certainly wasn't going to waste my time talking to her. I would give her the same cold shoulder that she was usually happy to give others when she felt in the mood.

I took the opportunity to approach Margaret when no one else was around and try and get her on-side with me about what a cold, stern, emotionless person Angela was. I said to her, "C'mon, you've got to admit she has a lot of horrible ways," but Margaret did not reciprocate my views. She said that was exactly the reason why she had thought of putting on something special at her house. She wanted the ill-spirit we showed to each other to change. Even though I complimented Margaret on how nice and approachable she was, she did not join in the negative attitude towards Angela. She told me I should accept people for who they were and not what I wanted them to be.

After that, I made an extra effort to have a conversation with Angela. She apologised to me for the times when she had been snappy and said it was no excuse but she had been going through a difficult time with her son, who was seriously ill, and she had been taking antidepressants because of it all. I saw that day there was more to Angela than met the eye and I confided in her about some things in my personal life too.

Margaret's plan had worked. We had timeout to have fun, kick back and relax and we all had a marvellous time. Margaret could have easily added more fuel to the fire over Angela, but she didn't, she chose to rise above it. Not only was she just a lovely lady, but she was also a wise one.

If we are not accepting of others how can we expect others to be accepting of us.

To work or not to work

I'm not working for the minimum wage. It's not worth getting out of bed for peanuts. I'll wait until something worthwhile pops up. I might as well stay on my benefits.

The Government are screwing the working class. I might as well chill at home, rather than do a job I don't want to do. I'm waiting for that astronaut's job to be advertised.

There are no jobs out there anyway. I never want to work.

Or on the other hand...

A job might do me the world of good. I would feel more confident about myself. My self-esteem would increase.

I would be busy doing something positive with my life. I'd be able to make a contribution towards my living.

I might even be able to afford to go out and socialise once in a while. I wouldn't feel as depressed if I was working; less time to focus on negative things.

I wouldn't have to be borrowing all the time. Finding work would improve my quality of life.

There may not be loads of jobs out there but if you're not looking, how will you find one?

Trivia

Glen: How are you?

Josh: I'm fine.

(I feel like shit!)

Glen: The weather's not so good today is it?

(I don't even know why I'm saying this)

Josh: No, it's meant to be non-stop rain.

(Like I care, if someone else mentions the weather again...)

Glen: How's Diane?

Josh: We're both great thank you.

(We are arguing all the time, in fact it's a real mess)

Josh: How are you and Theresa?

Glen: Yes, we're great too. She's just got promoted at work.

(We are no longer together, she won't even speak to me)

> *Sometimes it's appropriate to say nothing, but other times you miss an opportunity to say something.*

What's important?

What's important to you?

What means something to you?

Is it your job, your car, your other half?

What do you think about in your deepest thoughts?

What is it that counts, what's important to you?

Do you have any time to even consider what it is?

You can live and not know what drives you. I mean, not know what really drives you or what it is you're good at. You've got to try and carve something out for yourself, something you can do to bring you inner peace, regardless of anything or anybody.

What's important to you?

Still nothing?

You can't think? Okay, I'm going to approach this from another angle.

What is it that's *not* important to you?

Completing the counting for the stocktaking you still have to do at the weekend?

Listening to your brother-in-law explaining to you about the beauty of fly fishing for the fifteenth time?

Or cutting the hedges which still haven't been done yet?

You had no problem in mentioning those to me, did you?

Okay, let's try again. Let's turn it back around again.

What's important to you? Not anybody else, you. Still need some time to think?

You have a good ponder. If you find out what it is that's important to you, that's what you should be doing, because when we tap into the things that we find fulfilling, that's when we find contentment.

We can waste years and years doing things that aren't important to us.

What's important to you?

What can it do for you?

What can laughter do for you? What can a smile do for you? What can a pretty smile do for you? What can being yourself do for you? What can being open and honest do for you? What can being touched do to you? What can being loved do to you? What can being told you're special do to you? What can being accepted do to you? What can getting a compliment or being made to feel like you matter mean to you? What can, being appreciated do to you? Well if that's the case, then why can't we all do them a lot more often then?

I know what they can do for me. They can make me feel more confident about myself, make me feel stronger, give me a better outlook. They can make me feel like I'm on top of the world. And fill me up with good energy so I am able to tackle all the things that life can throw at me, and I know whatever happens I'll come through the other side because I've got so many good thoughts and people around me, things that keep me positive, things to keep me moving forward. So I guess I wanna thank you, because when you make me feel those things, I feel like I'm invincible.

Alone

I only left her for an hour or so. I used to shout upstairs from the front door before I went out, "I'll be back in an hour, Becky, don't forget to give her a kiss from Daddy." The neighbours praised me, called me a doting dad.

The Mrs and I had split up. She wanted out, so I told her, "You can go, you can do what you like, that's up to you, but Chelsea stays with me." She didn't put up a fight. She just took her belongings and went. People admired me for that, the fact I fought nail and tooth to have my kid. She wasn't fit to be a mother. She was no good. I knew Chelsea would have a better life with me. I'd have the odd hour or so down at the local on a night out to keep my spirits up. It was difficult being a full time mum and dad all rolled into one, but she was worth it.

I went down to the local for a drink with a few mates, Steven, Mark and Gareth. They were showing the footy on one of those big wide screen TVs. Champions League – Real Madrid v Barcelona. But when I was there, I had a fit. It was a pretty bad one too. I suffer with epilepsy you see. An ambulance had to be called and the medics started on me. Gareth told me, when I was coming around, he had tried phoning Becky my babysitter to tell her what had happened and to check Chelsea was okay, because he knew I'd be worried, but there had been no answer when he rang.

As soon as I came around and was alert again, I immediately told them all I was leaving. Gareth said he'd give me a lift home and come into the house with me and make sure Chelsea was okay. He thought I still looked very shaken and frightened. He said I had a look he hadn't seen before, but I told him to stay where he was.

When I got out of the pub, my heart was pounding like it was going to blow up. I ran home as fast as my legs would take me. I opened up the front door.

"Chelsea? Chelsea?" I couldn't hear a thing, no crying, not a thing. I closed my eyes and thought please let this be all right. I went upstairs to her cot. It wasn't good. It was an awful sight. Chelsea wasn't breathing. She had choked on her own vomit. She was... dead.

I had to admit it, when it all came out, I didn't have a babysitter. I don't know why I did it. Why I pretended I had someone looking after her. I just needed some time to myself and now Chelsea's gone. I wished I'd looked after her properly. *Don't risk it, do you hear me? Not even for five minutes. Even to nip down to the shop.* Cos you don't know what you'll be coming home to. I found out the hard way.

Non-stop

I have a few cans at the weekend, no big deal. It's all under control. I'm working, aren't I? Everyone has a drink, why don't they leave me alone? What's all the fuss about? So I sometimes have a drink during the week and occasionally I have a drink at work. Sometimes when I'm working nights it's a long shift, we all have a sneaky drink at work, don't we? You point the finger at me like I'm the only one. We all do it. And so what. I have a few drinks hidden out of sight, that doesn't mean I've got a problem. I only do it because you're always complaining you don't like to see me happy. Just because you don't drink, we all have to suffer because you're teetotal. You haven't got a happy bone in your body, you miserable twat. Well, I'm gonna keep drinking. It's cheap as anything at our local shop and no one's gonna stop me.

The other day, I heard that Phil Seton from round the Lakeside estate had passed away. He had a heart attack and he was fit as a fiddle, running marathons and everything. So what chance has any one of us got? Or, I read something in the paper; this lady had written something which has stayed with me which I'll never forget, about your lotto numbers coming up. I thought, I know what she means, none of us know when we're gonna die, when our number's going to be up. So I'm gonna enjoy my time whilst I'm here. Even with the threat of losing my life, or so the doctors claimed,

I was still drinking massive amounts. You might think I'm crazy, but I'm not, I'm an alcoholic.

End of the road

The tears roll down my eyes for you, the pain I feel is so strong it's hard to explain, I hurt so much, every part of me, I haven't been able to think straight since we parted ways. The reel of tape which held my feelings together has become unravelled, my heart isn't in sync any more and I just ache everywhere. Meanwhile you look better than you ever did. How is that possible, doesn't the end of us mean anything to you at all? You know I wished you were dead so the spell you have over me could be broken. Is that crazy that I love you so much it would be easier for me if you were dead? At least I would know you weren't still out there, somewhere in the world. They say the pain will go away; I hope so. I can't sleep, I can't eat, I can't function. I put a belt around my neck a few days ago and tightened it. After a few seconds I released it. Though it's not what I really wanted to do I just felt helpless and wanted the pain to stop so badly. You won't return my calls, you won't speak to me, why won't you just speak to me for five minutes, just so I can understand what happened and get my head around everything. That's all I asked for, I left messages, loads of messages, pleading with you to get into touch with me just for five lousy minutes. I told you I was going to see my doctor because of the break-up, I wasn't sleeping, I wasn't eating, I've not been able to go into work, I can't concentrate. Why won't you speak to me? I wished you had a heart, I know you have to be cruel to be kind but if you could just tell me what I did that has caused this I might be able to repair the damage. If I knew what it was I did that was so wrong I might be able to move on. I didn't do anything wrong. Didn't any of the time we spent together count for anything? I'm not getting any better, I'm getting worse. I used to love you, now I hate you. I still love you.

He's a wrong un

I told her he was the Devil reincarnated and he had beaten his last girlfriend so severely she had to be hospitalised; he was a monster. I thought she would fancy him as soon as she laid eyes on him, all the girls did. I blackened his name so she wouldn't look at him twice. Can you understand that he always looked so perfect, not a hair out of place, his physique, his smile. I said the things I did about him because surely no one would look at someone who could behave like that. But unfortunately on the one and only occasion when I couldn't be at her side because I had to be elsewhere she went to Christine Rodriquez's party and Stefan Jones introduced them to each other – my Eloise and him, in conversation. They started talking, she was wary of him at first but she had been drinking and you know what Dutch courage is like? She told him she didn't think much of him being a woman beater and all, but he asked her where she was getting all her information from and she let it slip that it was me who had told her. He corrected her and told her the truth: it was me who had half killed my girlfriend and it was me who had a violent nature and a history of beating my exes and two-timing them. And he told her to be careful. Everything I had said about him backfired and once the news was aired and my secret was out the more and more she probed and the more and more she found out. I really had changed from being that bloke I used to be but I still lost her. If I hadn't have opened up my mouth I'd probably still be with her. I didn't have to say anything about him, he didn't do a damn thing to me. I just saw him as a threat because he looked so sharp and pristine. I made out he was a shit for no real reason other than I felt insecure and ended up in the shit myself. When you try to flip shit on other people just be mindful the shit doesn't flip back on you.

Insecurity smothered with jealousy can be a venomous trait.

No not again

People have no idea what it's like. I booked a day off work last week to go to the optician. Everything was going fine, gorgeous day, no rain for a change. I got to the optician for my eye test, sat down, did what she wanted, Leanne I think she was called, I pressed my eye up against the lens like she told me to then I got that buzzing noise in my ears. That's how it always starts and straight away I was thinking oh shit, what's going to happen now. She said, "Are you okay Mr Williamson, you look to have gone a bit off colour?" I said I was fine but perhaps I could have a drink of water please. The voice in my head though was going ten to the dozen saying crazy random things like *fuck the bitch, just grab her.* Meanwhile I'm still talking to her pretending everything's normal. She was asking me to look into the light as she flashed her torch at me, to just focus on looking into the light, to open my eye wider for her. It was really difficult, picture yourself in that position trying to come off as normal. It wasn't unusual for me, just a typical day. But what if I hurt someone the next time? I'm afraid I might act upon what I'm hearing and do something I'll regret that'll get me put in a straight jacket for life. I'm back at work Monday. I am struggling though, I don't mind telling you. I had to investigate two dead prostitutes. The scene was all taped off, forensic teams everywhere, the two girls in question had been dead for a while, rigor mortis had already set in. There were a few at the scene who were crying, but not me, the voices were telling me jokes. I had to go to my car to keep my composure. Here I am at a crime scene, two dead bodies and I had to go to my car to stop myself from laughing, tears streaming down my eyes. I better go visit the doctor again. He's a friend of the family, he'll up the medication again I guess. Mental illness: who wants to admit to it? I'd be a laughing stock if it all got out and labelled a crackpot or relegated to a desk job, or worse have no job at all. No I'll keep shtum, especially in the position of authority I'm in. I've done twenty-five years in the force, my name is Geoffrey Williamson, Chief Inspector of the regional homicide team, ready and waiting for my next assignment. I showed a colleague from another department the last case we worked on and he said he was shocked how many leads hadn't been followed up on and he reckons if they were we cuda got a result. I don't know, I think he was a bit harsh in his findings, the bad guys don't always get brought down. I live in reality; you win some you lose some.

Hanging on

I threatened to take my life if she left me. I wasn't happy
the odd moment here or there but that's not the point, I'd
been with her for as long as I could remember, she was my
first and I swore she'd be my last. She broke down one day
and said she didn't love me any more, at least not how she
should do; she loved me like a brother. So I took a massive
overdose, I was admitted to hospital, and it worked out
– she came back to me. I knew she still loved me. Every
time she brought the subject up about finishing with me I'd
remind her what happened the last time she tried to break
up and we'd move on. I was still into her and she loved me.
Why else would she stay if things were that bad? For years
she told me she wanted out, said she wanted to be with
someone else and I should be with someone different too
but she still cared about me. I didn't want to hear about
her leaving and I always begged her to stay and we tried
again; sometimes she appeared to be happy then we would
be right back at the beginning again – she didn't want me,
it wasn't working, she didn't love me any more, blah, blah,
blah, blah. I think she was confused. I said if that's how
she felt I'd accept it for now but not for ever. I told her
I'd make her love me all over again, all she had to do was
give us a chance and we'd work it out. But she said she
was going whether I liked it or not and if I wanted to hurt
myself so be it, I was an adult, but she wouldn't be made
to feel guilty any more and she wouldn't be held to ransom

for one minute longer. So I cut my wrists. She didn't mean it, she came straight back to me. I think she just faced up to the fact that some people are just meant to be together. I mean if she didn't love me why on earth is she still here?

If you're not in a relationship by choice why are you there at all?

It's about you

Nick started to come out in red sores. His hands were all clammy, you could see the perspiration on him from a mile away, his shirts were wet through. He had certainly looked better in recent years. He was obsessed with his neighbours, he was always twitching and peeping out of the curtains to see if they had bought anything new. Why this worried him so much I do not know but it did. His sleep used to be good a while back but it was almost non-existent now and there he was back to the curtains again, up all night winding himself up: what have they gone and bought now, the show-offs? He just felt like he had failed his family and that he couldn't do anything right. He saw that his neighbour went on holiday three times a year while he could only afford to go once a year. His neighbour held a partnership at the firm he worked for while he was just an employee at his firm. He felt lousy about this; he was in a real pickle. A friend advised him to see his GP as he seemed to be down in the dumps most of the time and he reluctantly did, but after only a few minutes of giving the doctor a rundown of everything his GP told him he didn't need any medication as he was not clinically depressed like his friends and family had at first assumed. All he needed to do was stop focusing on his neighbours. He struggled in the beginning, telling his wife they were nothing special and yet look at them flaunting all their money. But when he was able to stop thinking about all the things they had and think instead about his own life he immediately started to feel better about himself, his whole outlook changed and he could recognise his own achievements. He was a good father and husband, he was kind and he was a good worker with an impressive record of attendance, and his opinion was respected by others.

Don't spend all your time looking at what your neighbours are doing. You can never know how they are doing, I mean how they are *really* doing. You only see a picture and pictures aren't always perfect are they? Feel a bit better now? There you go, I knew you would.

It's about how you are doing that counts. How are you doing?

All friends together

He came to my house when I was out most of the time. I never clicked. I know as I say it to you now you must think me a right fool – how could I have been so blind? But I didn't see it. He was sleeping with her for years basically, nearly as long as I was. I met her in April 2008 and they started sleeping together in November 2009. To top it all he was the best man at my wedding. Some of my so-called mates knew about it but not one of 'em told me; if they had have done I might have been able to stop it. They said they had realised what was going on but didn't feel it was their business to interfere. Stupid me, I thought friends were supposed to look out for one another. They talk about everybody else's business but when it came to mine they decided to adopt a code of silence, fucking hypocrites, I think they just wanted to see my head in bits. When it all came out one of the neighbours filled in the gaps. I found a pair of knickers in the back seat of the car. She said they were her Fiona's so I asked since when had her Fiona started saving her used knickers in my car and why would she have borrowed the car anyway when she didn't even drive. It made no sense. I pressed and pressed her, asked her to credit me with some intelligence. "Who is he? What's his name, c'mon Sheena? I'm not going to let it go." And she knew I wasn't after all the lies and tears and denials: the you don't trust me, you ought to be ashamed of yourself, how can you think I'd do something like that to you, are you going crazy. I still wouldn't let it go. Maybe it was through sheer exhaustion but eventually she confessed. And when she said his name well, oh my God, I could have passed out there and then on the spot. Patrick, Patrick? Not Patrick? Our Patrick? She said yes and it was like every part of me either collapsed or caught on fire. I'm sorry, I can't speak, you'll have to give me a minute... I asked her to break down every last detail to me, I wanted to hear it all, it was horrible but I'd been in the dark for so long I just needed to know. As it turns out Tanya, Jessie and Mandy, her so-called workmates, were really all him most of the time. He'd wait until my car had gone then she'd give him the signal which was to flick the light on and off to let him know the coast was clear, the children were in bed. Then he'd make his way into my house. They didn't care, they did it in our bed. I grew up with Patrick, he was like a brother to me. When the two people you love the most in the world do this to you, unless you've been through it, I can't explain it to you. It's left me numb. There is no limit or extent that some people won't go to get what they want, to satisfy their own needs. He could have met any woman, he chose my wife; and she could have met any bloke, but she chose my best friend. Be careful who you invite into your home and make sure the person you call a friend really is a friend. When I think about it now it is just as painful as the day I found out but at least I don't have to be there any more. If you take anything out of this you'll choose your friends carefully, come to think of it if you take anything out of this you'll choose who you fall in love with carefully too. It can start with a smile and a little bit of flirting and the next thing you know you'll be in my position; it's really that easy. What about your own relationship, what condition is that in?

Your best friend and your partner, do they get on well together? Have you noticed? That's good isn't it? Don't listen to me, it's probably all very innocent as these things often are. In fact I'm sure it is, it's just a friendship, isn't it?

Built to fall

This is a tale about Cuthbert Adams, a famous architect who lived in Scotland in the eighteenth century.

One thing he did have was an amazing ability to be able to see things what others could not see, he was indeed a true visionary. The buildings he designed were works of art: they were beautiful, and it was just a matter of time before he would become celebrated for them. The word spread far and beyond and soon everyone came to see his wonderful creations, and the buildings he had once just sketched were the toast of everywhere. They were breathtaking, simply marvellous, *bravo* everyone would say. Huge crowds gathered to witness his spectacular work but after seeing them countless times soon there was nothing new to say about them and everyone started to take his craft for granted. A well known writer had an idea: he said since there was nothing else to talk about perhaps people would be interested in other aspects of Adams' life, for instance that he was not able to maintain his marriage and his wife left him because he was impotent, or that he always had to have his lucky suit on before every drawing, or that he developed a peculiar stammer when nervous. Lucas, the writer, wrote the story and it had a great reception. The people wanted to know more and more about Cuthbert's private life. But soon there was nothing else to say so Lucas started inventing things. This hurt Cuthbert, who started to regret ever having been an architect; he hated all the publicity it had brought him, and it was painful for him to read ugly stories about himself. He had lost all faith: they had built him up to the sky only to pull him right back down to the bottom again. It was a cruel joke. Lucas himself did not like doing the stories: he knew they were untrue, but he justified his actions by saying the public had a thirst for them. Fast forward to the present day. These kinds of stories are still out there in the form of kiss'n'tell exposes, with estranged family and friends dishing the dirt for no other motive than wanting to tell the truth – nothing to do, of course, with any financial gain or payment they may receive. Sound familiar?

Just because you read it, that doesn't make it true.

Face value

I was with Sean for a while, all that time we spent together and when he dropped me he said I was uglier than his pitbull. Well that's how it all started, when I looked in the mirror and saw the reflection looking back at me I didn't blame him for saying all the awful things because deep down I'd always felt like he was out of my league and I was lucky to have him. I disgusted myself, I made a vow to change every single part of me from head to toe until I was beautiful enough to walk into a room and captivate absolutely everyone. And I wouldn't let money get in the way, I would spend whatever it took, whatever. The first thing I looked at was having my teeth done: over the years they had become yellow and stained and my two front ones made me look like Roger Rabbit. I got them fixed, that was £4,000. Then George came on the scene. He asked me to get a boob job, he liked big breasted girls, so I went from 32A to 36 double G – that was a whopping £8,000. He dumped me unbelievably for a girl with breasts no bigger than my original size. After that I met Rod and he asked me to get my nose done, said I would be dead pretty if my nose wasn't so big. So I did, it had to be broken in four separate places and rebuilt from scratch but the outcome was worth it; my nose was exquisite, it looked like a china doll's. That was £9,000 but he walked away too.

I was in a state of confusion, I wondered what it was I was doing wrong. I was jumping through all these hoops to please these men – sorry I mean for myself – and things were still going wrong. So I decided to have a complete makeover: I had my lips done, that was £3,000, my eyes were £6,000, my chin was £11,000, and I had fat drained from my legs which was £3,000. I had always hated my appearance, I just wanted to be loved. But after all the surgery I had even more problems. I was getting it all from all angles, most of them strangers, and they were calling me a freak show and said I belonged in a circus. On top of that I was skint, I didn't have a penny left, I'd got myself into so much debt in order to pay for the surgeries. But that's when I met Angus and put all of it behind me. It's five years now, no more operations, and I'm blissfully happy, cos I met a man who saw me for who I was and not what the plastic surgery made me look like. Perhaps the greatest change of all is I accept myself.

Super who?

I'm not a super hero, I don't have super powers, and I don't leap over buildings. I'm just a regular guy but today I did do something pretty amazing, if I say so myself. I saved seven lives. Something tragic happened but out of it came something so beautiful. I was walking up Baker Street. I had just bought a lottery ticket and a newspaper from the off-licence and I was on my way back home when I heard a loud screeching noise. I turned around but it happened so fast. A car mounted the pavement I was on, it was heading straight for me. You know when you want to do something but you can't, well that's what happened. I tried to move out of the way but I couldn't, I just froze. It hit me and swerved into a young mother who was pushing a pram beside me. There was blood splattered everywhere, needless to say neither she or her baby made it. I was lying on the floor with this acute thumping pain in my head; it got stronger and stronger, felt like a sledgehammer had just hit me, and then it felt like my brain was on fire. I was rushed to Accident and Emergency where it was discovered I had a bleed on the brain. In technical terms I had suffered a brain haemorrhage, amongst other injuries. I was wired up to loads of machines, I looked like an alien. When my family came to see me they hardly recognised me. They were in floods of tears. There was a CD player on the ward and they were singing my favourite songs, songs that had meant something to me at different stages of my life.

They were hoping for a miracle but the Chief Consultant at the hospital put an end to that. He gathered everyone together and broke the news to them that I wasn't going to come round and I would never be the same again. He was sorry but a stem check had revealed there was no activity, I was brain dead, it was just the machine keeping me alive. In his opinion it was time to switch it off and let nature take its natural course. He said he would give everyone a few minutes to consider what he had just said. There was an eerie silence, no spoken words at all, but everyone nodded their heads in agreement. He then asked if they would like to have my organs donated to help others who were at risk of dying and they told him they knew that was what I would have wanted. Now you see, like I said in the beginning, I didn't have a cape and I didn't fly around in the sky and I wasn't known across the world but I did save seven lives. Yes, I think I did something pretty amazing.

Outro

My state of mind when I wrote Wired Thoughts was very intense. There were occasions when I struggled to make the pen move, then at other times the concepts and ideas I had would appear one after another. When I was in that zone, it felt as though I was supposed to go down this path. Out of nowhere I decided one day I was going to write a book. I was relentless in my approach and attitude. As I wrote, one piece of work I would move on to another. I maintained that attitude from the beginning until the end. There were times I felt that what I was writing wasn't any good, when I would have what I would call my low confidence days, but when I was feeling good about myself I thought 'I'm going to do this. I really am going to complete this book and it's going to be good!' I just went up and down like this all the time, doubting myself, feeling good about what I was doing, then back to feeling like, 'Who am I kidding, will anyone be interested?' But some of the stories I wrote helped me to stay focused and to not lose faith, like Doubt for instance. So I stayed at the task and now the end product is here, so you can see for yourself, everything starts from a dream... you just need to have the desire and passion to see it through.

D R Dixon

Den Dixon does not have Doctorate or a Degree, he is not a motivational speaker, a professor, a therapist, a counsellor, an adventurer, a mountain climber or anything suchlike, as intriguing as these titles sound. To write, all you have to be able to do is write, so if you believe you have the ability, just let the pen hit the paper and see what happens.

Rest in peace

Stanley Gray and Georgianna Gray

Kenneth Dixon

Paul Lawrence and Jason Lawrence

Patrick Duggan and Jenny Duggan

Claude Patrice, Abtar Singh, Kevin Bent,

Joan Powell, Patricia Thomas and Terrie Peacock.